HOW TO WRITE FOR CHILDREN

For Peggy

With Best Wishes

Marion Hough

Swanwick '99

HOW TO WRITE
FOR CHILDREN

Marion Hough

WRITERS NEWS

THOMAS & LOCHAR

British Library Cataloguing in Publication Data
Hough, Marion
   How To Write For Children – (*Writers
   News* library of Writing; Vol. 8)
   I. Title II. Series
   808.06

   ISBN 0-946537-99-2 (hbk)
   ISBN 0-85877-000-9 (pbk)

Set in 11/12.5pt Sabon
by XL Publishing Services
Printed in Great Britain by BPCC Wheatons
for Thomas & Lochar
PO Box 4, Nairn, Scotland IV12 4HU

CONTENTS

CONTENTS

1
INTRODUCTION

Most of us have some experience of telling stories to children. Perhaps we are parents or grandparents, and have found ourselves telling bedtime stories to the young ones. Perhaps we have simply been babysitters, and have found that storytelling was the best way to keep the peace among fractious children.

The very fact that the children were an appreciative audience may have started us wondering: perhaps I could write stories for children? There must be lots of money to be made by writing children's books! Perhaps the idea just remained a daydream... something you will get around to doing one day. Or perhaps you really want to turn the dream into reality... and that is why you are reading this book.

Sadly, there are a number of things wrong with the daydream, a number of things that do not quite match up to real life. For a start, there is the little question of money. Yes, there are children's writers who are earning quite considerable incomes from their books. But not many children's writers get to be hugely rich: for most of us it is something from which we earn some money, but not a vast amount. The real reason we do it is not to get rich, but because we love the work.

The other problem with the daydream is that storytelling for an audience of family or friends is very different from writing commercially for an audience who has never heard of you. Your own children or grandchildren, or the children of people you know well, are on your side. They like you, and they are ready to like and enjoy any story you come up with. They will laugh with you, wonder with you, get excited with you, partly because you are you. But a printed book is not you; the printed page is there in between you and your audience, and you are going to need very real writing skills to bridge that gap.

However, the time you spent telling stories to children was certainly not wasted. Every children's writer needs to keep in touch with children, needs to sit down with them and to read to them and with them. That way you can understand what makes them laugh, what subjects fascinate them, and even what subjects frighten them. If you do not have children of your own, you would do well to borrow some: see if, for example, your local nursery school would welcome a spot of part time storytelling.

It is, though, a mistake to think of writing for children as being writing for one particular age group. The under fives, the 5 to 8-year olds, the 8 to 12-year olds, the young teens, the older teens; they are all different markets for the writer. Each group has different tastes, and uses a different vocabulary. Very few of us can write equally well for all of these groups. Generally speaking, our skills and inclinations will mean that we are better equipped to meet the demands of just one age group, and it is important to realise this.

Do also note that we have just talked about 'the demands of an age group'. Make no mistake about it, children are indeed a demanding audience for whom to write. They know what they like, and will quickly reject anything that does not meet their expectations. You will often hear an adult say of a book: 'it is a lot of rubbish really, but I am reading it through to the end.' You will never hear a child say that. If a child thinks a story is 'silly' he or she stops reading it at once.

In the US, they often describe writing for children as 'kiddylit'. It is a dangerous term to use, because it somehow suggests that writing for children is not real writing, that it is not just *for* juveniles but is actually juvenile itself. Nothing could be further from the truth: writing for children calls for writing skills of a very high standard.

So if you are going to get the most out of this book, you need to understand that writing for children is a demanding form of writing that you should only undertake because that is the kind of writing you really want to do. If you are in it only for the money, or if you do not have a proper understanding and respect for your audience, you are just not going to succeed. But if you have a proper respect for children and their tastes, and if you really want to write for them and to work for them, then you are about to explore the most fascinating of all forms of creative writing.

1
WHY WRITE FOR CHILDREN?

We find delight in the beauty and happiness of
children that makes the heart too big for the body.
Emersons *Illusion; The Conduct of Life*

Why write for children? Ask the question of a dozen children's authors and you could hear a dozen different answers. Most would agree it is certainly not because it is easier than writing for adults. It demands a different approach, a simplified vocabulary and an unshakeable belief that anything is possible. Above all, write for children because they are important to you.

RETURN TO YOUR CHILDHOOD

If you have a creative urge you should indulge it, work at it, enjoy it as does any artist. If, however, you intend to specialise in writing for the young, then recognise you are entering a world that is not new to you but probably long forgotten. You must realise that, as adults, many of us have allowed life's pressures to dull our emotional senses and reactions. We conform to what we consider to be adult behaviour, but if you are to communicate well you must perfect the art of remembering how it feels to be young, adventurous and vulnerable. You must try to recall the impact on you, the child, of various situations and your reactions to them. You must recall the extent your life seemed to be influenced or indeed ruled by adults.

Born to middle-aged parents and with a brother seven years older than myself, it was inevitable that, while my childhood was happy, I was at times a little lonely. I was, from the adult viewpoint, a solemn child. I earned the reputation of being an 'old-fashioned little thing' due to, I imagine, my obsession with games of pretence which, by my own choice, excluded the grown-ups but which allowed my colourful imagination to run riot. One of my earliest and favourite daydreams was, I am sure, a dire~t result of having listened to *Alice in Wonderland*.

As a very young child, I would imagine that I was a mere six inches tall and would prowl the house and garden on all fours, looking for adventure. A flight of stairs viewed from my imagined height presented an insurmountable obstacle, a crack or knothole low in the fence became a gateway to the unknown and next door's cat curiously peeping at me from the long grass, a terrifying creature in search of six inch prey.

Blessed with tolerant grandparents who were born storytellers, I made the most of the opportunity to establish my own identity, my own place in the family history, by listening to tales of 'the olden days'. Grandfather, a professional soldier in his youth, fuelled the fire of my imagination with sounds of drumming hooves, clashing steel, cracking rifles and the screams of the dying as their scarlet blood soaked the yellow sand of some far desert. Warning him that I would suffer nightmares if he continued to tell of such horrors, my gentle grandmother would turn the conversation to her own youth when, at the height of her beauty, she had sat for several portrait artists of the day. Transported unharmed from the field of battle, I listened to tales of old London as, with skill, she painted pictures in my mind of her own early years.

They told me of generations past, of my maternal greatgrandmother, the daughter of a French nobleman who married for love and spurned her father and the wealth that was rightly hers, of Uncle Fritz of German descent and a strongman in a travelling circus, who had captured the heart of Aunt Alice and whisked her away to lands unknown. My mind's eye saw the great moustachioed and muscled figure clad, I was assured, in nothing but an animal skin and sporting wide leather bands at each wrist. How my young heart understood why Aunt Alice had thrown caution to the winds and followed the circus and Uncle Fritz.

Stories of the seasons, hard toil and crop failure flowed from my father, born the youngest of a family of fourteen and raised a son of the soil, he would astonish me with his uncannily accurate predictions of the weather and animal behaviour. Never turning away my questions, he seemed to be a well of wisdom and knowledge.

The personal experiences of my mother, from high button boots to the days of the flapper, provided me with yet another fund of stories to which I could relate. Now, when they are all gone from this world, I realise how much they gave me, how they enriched my mind, each one leaving behind an impact of such strength that I can recall not only the stories they told but the childish excitement, fear, longing and tears which they evoked. A legacy of memories I put to good use when seeing a potential story through the child's eyes of my characters.

As a small child, one of my favourite Saturday morning treats was to visit the local market with my mother. I can still remember the mounting excitement as we threaded our way through the stalls offering a range of fresh produce, cakes, shoes, jewellery and clothing to the far end of the market, where sheep and cattle stood ready penned for auction. I was careful not to fidget or whine while my mother filled her basket with vegetables for the family, in the hope that eventually my patience would pay off. I knew that, when she was ready, my mother would accompany me to the shopping hall and the Aladdin's Cave of literature tucked into its far corner, the comic swap-shop.

The owner had an eagle eye for dog-eared or torn pages, for she paid only a percentage of the original cover price of each comic in strict accordance with its condition. With juvenile cunning, I regularly persuaded my mother to iron my weekly offering to ensure the highest price. Armed with a handful of coppers I was free to browse along the carefully stacked shelves for my favourite titles. I would return home impatient to immerse myself yet again in the adventures of *Desperate Dan* and *Keyhole Kate*.

My parents encouraged me to read anything and everything, often aloud, sharing with me my addiction to the written word and I was more fortunate than most in having a friend with American relatives. At regular intervals, they sent her batches of the latest colour comics and picture strip sections or funnies from their newspapers. This made her something of a celebrity among her peers; she was never short of friends and I made sure I remained one of them.

The tales of long ago bloomed again later in my life, nourished by the demands of my own children. They, too, were eager to establish their roots in family history and so enjoy a sense of belonging, an affinity with generations past.

Their memories are now added to my own for, in common with all children grown to adult life, they look back and with a seemingly superior wisdom, to compliment or criticise the decisions made by you, their parent. Sure that at the time everything was done for their own good, you are staggered to learn that a simple directive altered their lives in an heretofore undisclosed tragic manner, proving that, as a parent, you can never get it right. Think back to your own childhood and you will admit the truth of this statement that is repeated in each successive generation.

I believe, however, that when I planted the seed of influence governing my children's choice of books, I got it right. They both cut their reader's teeth on *Dr Seuss*, *My Naughty Little Sister* and dear old *Noddy*. Despite the little fellow's one time fall from grace, I am happy to report that neither my son nor daughter grew up to be bullies, racists or anything but healthily heterosexual. I am pleased to see that *Noddy* and kindly *Big Ears* are back in favour, albeit with a few minor adjustments.

My offspring went on to read for themselves such classics as *The Wishing Chair*, *The Famous Five*, *Swallows and Amazons*, *Clever Polly and the Stupid Wolf* and *The Lion, The Witch and The Wardrobe*. In later years, they turned their teenage minds to the world of comics, teen magazines and adult fiction. Novels written specifically for teenagers were scarce and, more often than not, their choice of reading matter was dictated by the reading lists from their English lessons at school. Today's child has a wide choice of books by new authors yet, time and again, the old favourites appear to delight the young imagination.

IDENTIFY WITH YOUR READER

Bear in mind, however, that children react differently from adults. It is not only a matter of perspective for, to a child of five the world is full of shoes and kneecaps, but emotionally too, for they have not yet learned the disciplines which govern adult behaviour.

Were you to step on the foot of an adult in a crowded bus, he would probably wince. He may even apologise for having put his foot in your way but not so with a child. A sharp yelp, an exaggerated grimace and a direct accusation would be the more likely result. A dim woodland path, inrushing tide, footsteps in wet sand may evoke only a passing interest from the adult mind, where to a child they can be the setting for the beginning of an adventure.

You must begin to look at things once again with the eyes of a child. When did you last really look at a butterfly, consider its method of flight, its lifespan, its delicate beauty? When did you last consciously listen to birdsong? When did you last stand on a station platform and watch the approach of a train, feel the rush of air as it passed you and consciously appreciate the sounds of slamming doors, calling guards and passengers embarking on their journey? Their journey to where? And why? And how? Or were you so concerned with your adult world that these small wonders escaped your notice?

DO NOT CONDESCEND

It is not, however, enough to be aware of these truths, it is also necessary to care deeply about the young lives which are influenced by today's writers. Do not write for children with a feeling of condescension, write with conviction, paying serious attention to your audience. Innocence is born again in each successive generation and is clearly seen in the eyes of the very young, those of the older child will show clearly his thirst of life, his doubts and his desire to learn. It is true to say that the emotions of a child are as far reaching as those of an adult, it is only the vocabulary with which to express them that is lacking.

Examples of the good, the bad and the downright unaccept-able can be found throughout children's literature in the work of authors both past and present. Perhaps one of the finest stories in which the writer honestly inhabits the world of the child is in Clive King's *Stig of the Dump*. In the following extract describing Barney's thoughts as he tumbles into Stig's pit, the author has expertly captured the imagination of a child when faced with a potentially dangerous situation:

> Barney wished he was at the bottom of the pit.
> And the ground gave way.
> Barney felt his head going down and his feet going up. There was a rattle of falling earth behind him. Then he was falling, still clutching the clump of grass that was falling with him.
> 'This is what it's like when the ground gives way,' thought Barney. Then he seemed to turn a complete somersault in the air, bumped into a ledge of chalk halfway down, crashed through some creepers and ivy and branches, and landed on a bank of moss.
> His thoughts did those funny things they do when you bump your head and you suddenly find yourself thinking about what you had for dinner last Tuesday, all mixed up with seven times six.

In a similar situation, an adult would probably begin assessing the possibilities immediately he began to fall. Broken limbs, brain damage or worse would probably be his first concerns, followed by the fear of being trapped and left undiscovered to die a painful, lonely death. Not so young Barney, however, with his childish confidence in the ability of the adult world to come to his rescue no matter what the situ-ation. He is far too curious about his new surroundings to worry about something so trivial as injury to himself.

The same innocent curiosity is displayed when, having

matter-of-factly discovered that he is not dead but tangled helplessly in creepers on the face of the cliff, Barney realises he is not alone:

Barney decided he wasn't dead. He didn't even seem to be very much hurt. He turned his head and looked around him. It was dark in this den after looking at the white chalk, and he couldn't see what sort of a place it was. It seemed to be partly a cave dug into the chalk, partly a shelter built out over the mouth of the cave. There was a cool, damp smell. Woodlice and earwigs dropped from the roof where he had broken through it.

But what had happened to his legs? He couldn't sit up when he tried to. His legs wouldn't move. Perhaps I've broken them, Barney thought. What shall I do then? He looked at his legs to see if they were all right, and found they were all tangled up with creeper from the face of the cliff. Who tied me up? thought Barney. He kicked his legs to try to get them free, but it was no use, there were yards of creeper trailing down from the cliff. I suppose I got tangled up when I fell, he thought. Except I would have broken my neck if I hadn't.

He lay quiet and looked around the cave again. Now that his eyes were used to it he could see further into the dark part of the cave.

There was somebody there!

Or something!

Something, or Somebody, had a lot of shaggy black hair and two bright eyes that were looking very hard at Barney.

'Hullo!' said Barney.

Something said nothing.

'I fell down the cliff,' said Barney.

Somebody grunted.

'My name's Barney.'

Somebody-Something made a noise that sounded like 'Stig'.

'D'you think you could help me undo my feet, Mr. Stig?' asked Barney politely.

15

Barney's lack of fear stems largely from his child's view of danger and death, so skilfully conveyed by the author, as a fact of life uncomplicated by grief or pain. Shielded, as they so often are, from the true emotions of their parents during times of upheaval – the death of a grandparent, job loss, serious accident or illness – children invariably face potentially dangerous situations without preconceived ideas of the possible consequences and often, therefore without fear.

On a lighter note, Nina Bawden's *Peppermint Pig* contains a graphic description of a child's horror of being expected to wear an unsuitable garment to school guaranteed to wring a long-forgotten but hatefully familiar churn to even the most world-weary adult stomach:

A week passed – and something much worse did happen to Theo than being teased by Noah Bugg. Aunt Sarah knitted him a pink woollen vest and he had to wear it to school.

It was made of thick, soft wool and knitted in a pretty lacy pattern. Mother said, 'Sarah must have sat up till all hours, it is good of her. She says she'll have another one ready by the time this one needs to be washed.' She saw Theo's sickly grin and added in a coaxing voice, 'Your Aunt Sarah is worried about you getting a chill, this bitter cold weather.'

'I'd rather get a chill than wear that,' Theo said, 'It's a girl's vest. I'd rather die.'

He meant it: he felt really desperate. Mocking laughter filled his dreams; tormenting boys danced round him gimlet-eyed. 'We can see what you're wearing, Baby Theo Greengrass!' He prayed for a miracle – for the house to burn down and the hateful vest with it while they were all safely out – but his prayers were not answered. The first day of school, the humiliating garment was laid out on the chair at the end of his bed. He put it on and came down to breakfast wishing the earth would open and swallow him.

Polly tried to comfort him, 'No one will see the vest under your clothes. No one will know.'

'I'll know!' He pushed the porridge round his plate, the tears springing.

It is a very fortunate child that has never been forced to wear something he knows will make him a laughing stock of the school. Not only does the author effectively build up the child's misery, she also skilfully incorporates that awful sinking feeling you experience when you know the adults have no intention of relenting and you have no choice but to wear the hateful thing.

Acknowledge that to write for children, you must develop an awareness of what will best feed the imagination in the growing mind and develop the ability to use simple inspired language which has strength, wastes nothing and needs no lengthy explanation. Direct questions such as 'We know children don't we?' and 'Wasn't he a naughty boy?' are unacceptable to today's young reader and set up an automatic 'us and them' barrier between the writer and the child.

The influence of the classic tale

Whilst the trend in today's books for children is far removed from the archaic language and small print of standard classic tales, a quick glance at the storylines will reveal plenty of clearly identifiable similarities.

Old favourites such as Rudyard Kipling's *Just So Stories* and A.A. Milne's *Winnie The Pooh* are prime examples of the moral tale. Ignore your parent's warnings about naughty behaviour at your peril.

When Kipling's trunkless *Elephant Child* pestered his relations with his 'satiable curiosity', even numerous spankings failed to deter his quest to discover what the crocodile had for dinner. His eventual brush with the crocodile made him a sadder, wiser and far longer-nosed creature. In other words, 'mind your own business'.

Nesbit's *Railway Children* having proved itself an enduring favourite with young readers, went on to become a hit at the cinema box office with successive generations. Its main appeal must lie in its message of a family winning through together against apparently insurmountable odds. But even here, the hint of a natural phenomena seen through the eyes of the child and translated into magic was not forgotten, as in this excerpt when the trees begin to slide down the railway embankment:

> And, as Peter pointed, the tree was moving – not just the way trees ought to move when the wind blows through them, but all in one piece, as though it were a live creature and were walking down the side of the cutting.
> 'It's moving!' cried Bobbie, 'Oh look! and so are the others. It's like the woods in Macbeth.'
> 'It's magic,' said Phyllis, breathlessly, 'I always knew the railway was enchanted.'

Despite the disadvantage it could have suffered from being a set school English reader, Kenneth Grahame's *Wind In The Willows* must be the blueprint for just about every woodland story ever written. Descriptions of woodland life provide the perfect backdrop for the awful, greedy but loveable rogue Mr Toad, sensible Ratty, bumbling Mole and wise old Badger. The introduction of the evil weasels, a fierce battle, Toad learning his lesson and Rat and Mole finding their way safely home again combine all the ingredients of adventure, excitement and a moral, happy ending so essential in children's fiction.

With *Mary Poppins*, author P.L. Travers invented the definitive 'good fairy' to rescue the children from unfeeling, insensitive parents. Although technically an adult, her magical powers lifted her above the restrictive regime under which the children were required to live and provided an escape route for their emotions and imagination which helped set everything right.

Peter Pan and *The Lion, The Witch and The Wardrobe* share the same moral message of good triumphing over evil. J.M. Barrie and C.S. Lewis both use one of the techniques most appealing to the young reader of allowing the children to take control of how they defeat the enemy and save the day, with the 'adult' figures put into the book purely as guides to the best paths to follow. Once again, the message must be, 'follow the advice of those older and wiser and you won't go far wrong.'

These much loved, familiar plots are as good today as they ever were. Updated, they can be reworked to delight a new generation of young readers.

In its role as the definitive woodland tale, the basic story-line of *Wind In The Willows* would happily stand modernisation. An up to the minute version could recast the weasels as a mutated species of super rodent introduced to the wood and threatening the balance of nature. The introduction of a strong conservation theme with Ratty, Mole, Badger and Toad not only fighting to restore the status quo but representing all endangered species, directs the story right to the heart of the conservation conscious child.

Fantasy dreams of the type depicted in Lewis Carroll's *Alice in Wonderland* have always held enormous potential for the would-be children's writer. Today's Dormouse could be a small alien, Mad Hatter a space scientist and instead of sending the White Rabbit down into the bowels of the Earth to reach his Wonderland, in the new version he could find himself cast in the role of an astronaut, leading a jean clad, tee-shirted Alice to a Wonderplanet circling high above the Earth.

In *The Wishing Chair*, Enid Blyton provided her young readers with a conscious projection into the world of adventure. By replacing the chair with a desktop computer, the high-tech youngster will happily relate to a story that allows him to explore the full extent of his imagination.

In her timeless book, *The Borrowers*, Mary Norton proves that fairies always have, still do and always will live at the bottom of the garden. They may be called something quite different, they may not have wings or cast magic spells but children still believe in the undeniable existence of a parallel world inhabited by 'little folk'. Having been discovered by 'the boy' Borrower Arrietty is astonished that he should mistake her for a fairy and he, in turn, is concerned to be seen still believing in such things:

He stood a moment, as though embarrassed, and then he said: 'Can you fly?'

'No,' said Arrietty, surprised, 'Can you?'

His face became even redder, 'Of course not,' he said angrily, 'I'm not a fairy.'

'Well, nor am I,' said Arrietty, 'nor is anybody. I don't believe in them.'

He looked at her strangely, 'You don't believe in them?'

'No,' said Arrietty, 'do you?'

'Of course not!'

Write because you care

It is obvious that these authors and many like them cared deeply for the children for whom they wrote, as should you. If social and emotional equality existed among today's children, it would hardly be necessary to write this book for there would be only one market for which to cater but as in the adult world, modern day stress can affect even the youngest mind. Today's freedom, however, for a writer for children, allows him to explore subjects which have, until recently, been considered taboo. It is easy to immerse oneself in Dickensian fiction, consoling your conscience that children are no longer forced to suffer the hardships experienced by David Copperfield and Oliver Twist. Sadly, however, the caring writer is forced to come to terms with the fact that many of today's children live in a world troubled by social deprivation, abuse, drugs, racial prejudice, pollution and broken homes. As writers, we must not only recognise these elements but handle them in a responsible manner: a difficult area and one that will be explored thoroughly later in the book.

On a lighter note, you will need a bright and lively imagination, a keen sense of humour, a great deal of patience and finally, a certain clarity of mind which will enable you to filter the puns, sarcasm, catchphrases and jokes which, while they are part of your adult understanding, will mean nothing to the young reader. Those bedtime stories you used to make up for your children may initially have triggered your desire to write but be prepared to alter them considerably before trying your luck with a publisher.

The imaginary creatures, talking animals and dream homes which, stamped with your own beloved and highly identifiable maternal or paternal personality, were compulsive listening to your nearest and dearest, will find far less favour with the public at large.

Those pet names, hilarious family jokes and holiday stories mean nothing to the average child in the street, so when close relatives and friends urge you to, 'write that down and put it in a book for children', bear in mind that it's not as simple as it seems.

EMOTIONS ONLY LACK VOCABULARY

Recently, in conversation with a good friend, she remembered that an experience at the age of three made such an impact that, some forty years later, she can still recall and relive the emotions she felt. A minor injury caused her to attend the accident department of her local hospital. Her mother had bought her a comic to read while she waited in the casualty department and when she was taken for treatment, the nurse put the comic away for safekeeping.

Treatment completed, the nurse held the comic at arm's length with the words: 'Here's your comic. Now, what do you say?'

My friend, naturally shy and still shaking from her ordeal, whispered a thank you and waited expectantly but to no avail as the nurse had simply not heard the child's response. To her dismay, my friend saw the nurse stiffen and frown, adamantly refusing to give up the comic until she was thanked in the proper manner. Not until the child was reduced to tears, did her mother intervene to restore the comic to its rightful owner. As my friend explained, her mother was so concerned to have her child seen as the model of politeness and good behaviour, that her naturally protective instincts were temporarily overridden, leaving her tiny offspring feeling powerless, frustrated and so furiously angry at the injustice of the situation, that those feelings have remained with her to the present day.

Sadly, incidents such as this have the potential to rupture the umbilical cord of trust between child and adult. In a similar incident, a male relative now approaching his sixties, recalled having been forced to spend time in hospital at the age of four and having been showered by friends and relatives with a variety of new toys. His resentment at having been forced on his release from hospital to leave everything behind for the benefit of the other children, has not only remained with him throughout his life but he feels, has been responsible for his often lavish and ill-affordable gifts to his own children. Had he been able to voice his feelings at the time and to have that voice heard by the adults governing the situation, would he have been influenced in later life to compensate the frustrated child within him by over-indulging his own offspring?

The lesson to be learned by the children's author is that the strength and breadth of a child's emotions should not be underestimated but regarded as an important factor in the growth of the child.

By now you will have realised that the craft of writing for children, in common with the young mind, is more complex than you may, at first, have imagined. The next step is getting to know your reader.

2
GETTING TO KNOW YOUR READER

*Children are remarkable for their intelligence
and ardour, for their curiosity and intolerance of shame,
the clarity and ruthlessness of their vision.*
Aldous Huxley *Vulgarity in Literature*

A report highlighting the benefits of pre-natal contact between mother and child stated that during pregnancy should the mother-to-be regularly read aloud specific nursery rhymes and stories and sing simple children's songs the child, once born, would show a marked preference for those particular songs and rhymes.

Coincidence or pre-natal influence? Should it prove to be the latter, it poses the question, at what stage does the young mind begin to absorb the teaching of the world in which it lives?

Most adults will have wondered and exclaimed over the reactions of a tiny infant to the early games of Peep-Bo, the foot straddling Ride-a-Cock-Horse, or the toe-tweaking This Little Piggy Went to Market. After playing the game only a few times, the toddler's face registers delight in anticipation of each tweak or tickle, clearly denoting an early learning ability. Some five year olds, due to tuition by a parent or older child, arrive in the classroom already capable of reading simple sentences while others, for no apparent reason, continue to struggle with the written word for several years.

The firstborn of a family will often apparently progress quickly due to the constant and adoring attention of parents, grandparents and friends, while a second child will appear slow by comparison. I once knew a particularly inarticulate three year old boy, who spoke nothing but 'scribble'. His worried parents relied on the older sister, an extremely bright girl of five, to translate his every need. On examination, their family doctor pronounced the younger child perfectly normal and forbade the little girl to act as a go-between. Within three or four frustrating and tearful weeks, the three year old began, out of need, to speak clearly. He had learned a basic vocabulary but with his sister to rely upon, had found no need to use it.

As in all good stories, there was of course a happy ending. Both children exhibited a similar standard of intelligence and ability in later years, with the wonderful bond between them continuing into adult life. If two children in one family can, in their first few years, respond and develop so differently, how then can we, the writers, clearly define the ages for which we cater?

The answer is that there is no such clear definition, there must be an overlap, an allowance for ability within each age range. An intelligent six year old is capable of enjoying a story written for older readers, while a slow learner will continue into his teens to read those tales designed for children younger than himself.

LEARN TO LISTEN

I will happily confess to a weakness for children under the age of six or seven, for their minds are still alive with unspoiled magic. Creating books and stories in both text and picture strip for this age group is one of the most enjoyable and absorbing aspects of writing for the world of children.

As a young mother, one of the nicest moments in my day was when, at around 7 o'clock, my little rascals were tucked into bed and begging for a story. It gave me the self-indulgent chance to weave a tale of magic or adventure for my wide-eyed offspring. When, in later years, I came to write for children though, I realised that appreciation shown by one's own children does not necessarily mean success with the publisher.

In telling stories to my own children, I had been aware of

what might please or frighten them, the words and simple plots they would be able to comprehend. They were average children but once I began to write, I realised that I could not assume that all youngsters progress at the same rate, it was essential therefore for me to really get to know and genuinely like my potential reader.

Children, you will by now have noticed, come in all shapes and sizes and it is possible that you have some of these small folk actually living under the same roof as yourself. Until now, you might have thought that, whilst you rightly consider yourself blessed, they constitute at times some sort of nuisance. If, however, you intend to write for children, then you have a wonderful opportunity to study your reader at close quarters. Next time they are squabbling among themselves, stop and listen to the vocabulary, to the logic behind their argument. Discover the root cause of the problem, it may seem minor to you but it could be of gigantic proportions to the younger mind. Estimate who is likely to be the victor and why, the final outcome may surprise you, if of course you have not found it necessary to step in before there is a blood bath. Their properties are of a different quality to your own, and to achieve them they will apply a subtle pressure perfected in youth.

Children are born manipulators, in order to achieve their heart's desire and dependant upon their environment and method of upbringing, they will approach the challenge along avenues that you, the adult, would not even have considered. Many years ago on BBC Radio's *Children's Hour*, Uncle Mac would end his programme by saying: 'Goodnight children, be good but not so terribly good that someone says "And now what have you been up to?"' A child who willingly tidies a bedroom, washes up or takes the dog for a walk without being asked is, of course, possibly a virtuous youngster – but more probably he is laying down the groundwork for a well thought out plan of campaign.

Ask yourself how recently you can recall a situation where you have willingly purchased an expensive item for a child which perhaps you could ill afford, nonetheless convinced it was undeniably needed or deserved. Now, consider the sequence of events leading to the purchase, who persuaded you into that line of thought and with subtlety, influenced your final decision?

'But Mum, all my friends wear make-up. Why can't I?'

'Dad, the whole class are going to Austria and I can borrow a pair of skis, so it won't cost much!'

PEER PRESSURE

Children are born 'wannabees' yet at this stage in their growth, it is as much a need as a desire to possess the accepted symbols relevant to their age group. Each generation has its own fashion requirements most of which, due to demand, are highly priced.

The school plimsoll, in recent years, has been replaced by a range of expensive trainers. No child of today would choose to be caught by its peers without at least one pair of jeans bearing the essential label in their wardrobe, and a trip to the hairdresser and the child's demand for a fashionable cut and style will make the average parent blanche at the cost.

Parental opinion is divided at this point. On the one hand, the child should be made to recognise the value of money and on the other lies the conviction that peer pressure can damage the emotional stability of the young mind.

Many parents, dimly remembering the needs and desires of their own formative years, will somehow find the money to furnish their child with the necessary trappings of youth, the uniform which will make them acceptable to the rest of the herd.

The adult mind is forced to accept that at a very young age children can find themselves, through circumstances, firmly established as either haves or have-nots. Their membership of one group or the other is not necessarily governed by finance alone. It can often be due to a lack of parental understanding, physical disability or even something as simple as a dialect alien to that of their peers.

You may not, however, be fortunate enough actually to live with children in your house. This means you need to borrow other people's, and one tried and tested method is the offer to babysit for friends and neighbours. There is an old Danish proverb which says: Who takes the child by the hand takes the mother by the heart. Not only will you very quickly acquire a circle of young friends who will provide you with a fund of information about the young mind, but you will also have the opportunity to talk to the children in your care. I do not advise starting with babies in cots as their conversation is limited. However, children from three years onward, once you have won their confidence, will talk at great length about anything and everything. Your main problem will be actually getting them to bed, which usually can be achieved by the promise of a story, hopefully constructed from your own imagination. Do not be upset if your audience falls asleep halfway through. It is not a critical appraisal, it is merely that nature has taken over.

Of course, babysitting is not necessarily confined to the evening hours. Many young mums welcome an afternoon or morning off, enabling them to visit the hairdresser, go shopping for that new dress or simply to put their feet up with a cup of coffee. Once you have established a relationship of trust with both the child and the parent, offer to take little Simon or Karen to the park for the morning or perhaps a more exciting trip to a local fair or zoo. At all times be aware of your responsibilities but take the opportunity to watch the child at play, to observe facial expressions when the youngster is confronted with something new, exciting, fearful or sad and above all listen to the account of the outing delivered to the parent upon its return.

Dialogue in anything written for children must be authentic and you must learn to take every opportunity to eavesdrop. Mingle with the young mums when they go to collect their children from primary school. While you are waiting outside the gates, listen not only to the conversations of the mothers who are waiting for their offspring but to the children as they come racing out, brandishing pictures they have drawn destined to be pinned up on the kitchen wall, letters from teachers and articles of clothing they have not quite managed to scramble into. Listen carefully to their first words. Did they have a good day or a bad day? Do not think that privilege is confined to adult life. What went right? Did they get a star? Did they get a good mark for reading or did they argue with their best friend or get ticked off by their teacher? Whatever the issue, listen to the words they use. Remember, a child's vocabulary is limited but their emotional range is the same as that of an adult.

AGES SIX AND UPWARDS

Sadly, this unrestrained joy of life begins to disappear as they become older, when they become more reticent in their approach to adults, unwilling to reveal too much of themselves for fear of misunderstanding or outright criticism. There is and always has been, when compared with other age groups, a shortage of good material for readers between the ages of six and ten, for this is perhaps the most difficult group for which to write. Once a child begins to attend school, much of what it came to accept in its first five years as truth becomes subject to doubt. Belief in Santa Claus, the tooth fairy and magic in general is slowly eroded, despite the child's wistful and secret desire to cling to such comforts.

A new world is theirs, one with which they must come to terms in their own way, new classroom disciplines, acres of new knowledge to be absorbed, hundreds of new relationships to be forged and with it all occurs the herd instinct, a need to be acceptable to one's peers.

Loving parents will often tell you these are the first of the difficult years. Behavioural patterns alter, carefully taught diction disappears overnight and tastes in reading material begin to mature. The world of comics produces some admirable weeklies for this age group, concentrating mainly on television characters, slapstick humour, simple craft articles and items of general interest. Books range from the first reader, incorporating a simple vocabulary and colourful illustrations to animal tales, adventure, school stories, nonsense yarns and juvenile humour usually produced in larger print with black and white illustrations.

Entry into the junior school, for the eight to eleven year

age group, is yet another milestone. With it comes the pressure of end of term tests and, dependent upon the policy of the individual school, the first lessons in a foreign language (and in some cases, homework). Pressures too from their peers, a 'keeping up with the Jone's syndrome occurs. Clothes, toys, freedom to stay up late, go out unaccompanied with their friends, involvement in sports and a need to voice their opinions colour each day, causing the beginning of conflict with adults responsible for their safety and education.

You train them in road safety and self-assurance, only to have to watch, white knuckled with fear, as they set out for the local park. Inevitably, this lies at least three major roads away and your child is going off unaccompanied, except for the equally diminutive figure of their best friend and his marginally older sister. If you intend to write for this age group, it is essential that you indulge in some in-depth market research.

Schools can play a very important part in your research into the mind of a child no matter what age. Contact the head teacher at your local infant and junior school and offer your services as a story reader. Many schools welcome this approach with open arms, affording as it does the opportunity for the teacher to use the time allowed in preparation for the next lesson or in marking books. Once you have the necessary permission, you can sit and read to a class of fascinated children as they sit wide-eyed, open-mouthed and hopefully, in blessed silence. Once you have established a good rapport with the school it is often possible for you to suggest a longer session from which both you and the children will derive benefit.

My contact with schools began when I was invited along for a whole day working in the morning with the five to seven year olds and after lunch with the eight to elevens.

At first, I found it terrifying to be faced with two hundred or so children sitting cross legged in rows on the floor of the main hall, their faces turned upward, daring me to fail their expectations of relief from classroom tedium.

Not quite so daunting now but always filled with surprise,

my days at school have come to bring a sense of enjoyment, for here are my readers, eager not only to be amused but unwittingly to help me with my own market research.

Begin by reading aloud a story suitable for the age group concerned. The next step is to call for volunteers to state whether they liked or disliked the tale and why. Initial reticence soon gives way to a forest of hands, for most children love to be heard. An analysis of the writer's work then follows, establishing clearly the central character, their problem and the solution. Then comes the best part of the exercise. By leading the now enthusiastic young listeners gently through the maze, they volunteer their own choice of character, fleshing it with a name, mannerisms and family background. An accepted truth that characters make plots leads them naturally on to pinpoint a suitable problem for which they then offer a solution. The clever part is to know which suggestion for a character to select from the hundreds received in order to be able to steer their enthusiasm and to mould the finished work into an acceptable story. They enjoy an hour or so's unrestrained fun, little realising the wealth of knowledge and understanding that I take away with me after every visit.

After consultation with their teachers, children between eight and eleven are often asked to complete the story during a subsequent lesson. On these occasions, the formula is as before but they are left at the point where the central character has yet to solve the problem. The completed stories are collected and sent on to me by the teaching staff for my appraisal. This allows me a wonderful insight into the ingenious mind of a child proving their preference for happy and surprise endings. I make sure I return to the school within a week or so to congratulate and present prizes of books to the three best writers.

Book weeks are held at most schools throughout the year, giving the student an opportunity either to listen or discuss with a local writer the variety of literature available to today's reader. Never pass over an invitation of this nature as it will afford a rare insight into the complex world of the young adult.

The child, by now, is well aware of many forms of conflict whether in the home or in the society in general. A dimly heard minor argument between parents can assume terrifying proportions in the mind of a child, heralding the possibility of divorce and the destruction of their security, a security already threatened by half understood warnings to avoid talking to strangers, by television reports of atrocities inflicted upon individuals and nations alike. Theirs is rapidly becoming a world in which theft, assault, abuse, deprivation and death must be acknowledged. It falls not only to parents and educators but also to writers to introduce these subjects (in which so often the child is the victim) in a manner which serves to increase the child's understanding without causing the reader to become obsessed with the ugly side of life before they have experienced the joys of living.

Much is learned in these years which is character building. Children are often encouraged to take part in fund raising events, expending effort and deriving a sense of achievement by helping those less fit or fortunate than themselves. Often they establish an interest in clubs, brownies, a church organisation, hobbies or sports, discovering more each day about themselves and the world in which they live.

This, as most parents know, is the period when whatever you do, for whatever reason, later in life, your children will tell you, you got it wrong. In their early years, you encouraged them to think for themselves and to draw their own conclusions. At the age of seven or eight, you find you have to listen to them confidently voicing their opinions each day.

ADOLESCENTS AND YOUNG ADULTS

At eleven, another trauma, a change of school and the need to re-establish their identity. Having worked their way to the top of the junior school with, often in their last year, the responsibilities of a prefect, they find themselves on the lowest rung of a new order.

Here, the opportunity to mature physically and emotionally appears limitless but with it comes added responsibility for their own actions. Interests in literature must, on the one

31

hand, encompass 'required reading' by the school, but on the other can begin to exhibit a fast-growing commitment to personal preference. Many young people between the ages of eleven and thirteen make the leap to the adult book world with its often lurid jackets and devalued concepts in an effort to appear worldly-wise among their friends. This is the time when sex becomes an issue of importance, when girls giggle and fantasise about boys and when boys are faced, at nature's command, grudgingly to admit that girls are not as daft as they seemed a year or so earlier.

The search for realism in the written word was at one time confined to the adult novel. Nowadays it is dealt with in a responsible manner by many authors in books designed specifically for this age group, which can be found in not only county but school libraries the length of the country.

By fifteen, puppy love romance and choose your own adventure has been left behind, replaced by, here and there, an interest in the classics, although research has proved beyond doubt that few books in this category are bought by the young reader, normally they are purchased by a nostalgic adult in the form of a gift. Rather interest turns now to the real adult novel, where either a slice of life, historic or modern, real life adventure, science fiction, political intrigue or social injustice governs the final choice.

Romantic fiction for the young teen has altered its image to relate to today's values, for by now they have ceased to snigger over sex and have begun to acknowledge its place in the importance of a relationship. Of far greater value to the reader is the exploration of personalities and loyalties, an everyday exercise whether at play or at school.

ACHIEVERS, LEADERS AND LATE DEVELOPERS

Any parent of two or more children will tell you, to their own confusion, that their offspring are totally unalike in anything but a physical family resemblance. One child may be docile, obedient and trouble-free from toddler to teens, while the other, inexplicably since it has been subjected to an identical upbringing, will be fractious, disobedient and troublesome

32

throughout its young life. Closer examination of such circumstances may possibly reveal hidden factors pertinent to that specific family, yet some of the basic causes of the differences seen in the behavioural patterns of children born to the same parents often have their roots in the family pecking order.

Detailed university studies have, for example, discovered that in small families, the oldest child exhibits a relatively high IQ, benefiting undoubtedly from the constant attention and encouragement offered to the newborn by its doting first-time parents. Every moment of its life is the subject of concern or approval. Its first words are greeted rapturously, its first step, a milestone of achievement and the opportunity for a little parental boasting. An unfortunate legacy for the eldest child, however, was also revealed by the study that, in later life, they are often prone to stress-related ailments.

The birth of a second child to the family, if it occurs within three to five years of the first, brings with it a change in parental behaviour, which reflects in the pattern of the child's upbringing. With each new arrival, the amount of time given to parenting must be shared equally throughout the brood. Consequently, while the child may be welcomed and loved to the same extent, the milestones which won such acclaim in the first child, do not engender the same feeling of wonder and congratulation in the second infant. Disappointment may even be felt by the parent when, subsequently, the second child does not achieve at the same speed as the first. Usually, the loving parent is totally unaware that this disappointment is being relayed to the understanding of the child.

Small wonder, then, that the younger child, in many cases, lacks the desire to excel if, from the outset, it feels marked down as an under-achiever.

The sex of a child, however, can play an important role. If the second or third child is the opposite sex to its siblings, then it is more likely to benefit from the same attention as a firstborn. This, in fact, was the case in my own family. My brother, seven years my senior, had enjoyed the attention paid to a first child long before I came on the scene. My father, I have been told, was overjoyed at the birth of a daughter and I, too, had firstborn attention lavished on me.

If I look back to any stage in my childhood, I remember my brother as being, at times, my champion and friend and at others, distant and uninterested but at no time, a close companion. The age gap, in fact, did not disappear until we were both well into adult life and married. His years spent as an only child, I am sure, played an important part in our adult relationship. For seven years, he had enjoyed the benefits of not having to share his parents' time or praise with another child. In many ways, he was sheltered from having to give way or make concessions and I feel sure that whilst, initially, his baby sister afforded no threat to his existence, he must to some degree have felt resentment at my arrival.

An isolated only child is a sad figure and a wise parent ensures that, from an early age, it becomes involved with other children, either with the greater family or by attending playgroups or nursery schools. This way, the only child benefits from social interaction.

Bearing in mind this pecking order, it is clear that one child within the family will emerge as a leader. Whilst there are other attendant factors, early acquisition of the skills of leadership normally occurs in the home. An attractive, outgoing child with a sense of adventure will quickly become such a leader among his peers. Such children are invariably chosen as class monitors or team leaders, are invited to parties and everybody wants to be their friend.

Less fortunate is the late developer or sadly, the child who is rejected by the herd on the strength of a minor abnormality. This could be physical, such as a birthmark, slight limp or obesity; social due to a disadvantaged home background or, even in this day and age, the problem could have racial roots.

These differences often lead to the victim being bullied and a subsequent loss of self-esteem. Unlike the natural leader, these under-achievers are always the last to be picked for a team, nobody attends their parties and they are usually to be found standing on the sidelines, wistfully looking on as life's opportunities pass them by.

LOOKING THROUGH CHILDREN'S EYES

Think back once again to your own childhood and you will find that basically, children's tastes today vary only a little. They still like a story with a beginning, middle and an end. Under seven year olds continue, like myself, to believe that fairies and other little folk are alive and well and in all probability, living at the bottom of the garden.

The process of getting to know your reader is essential and if imaginatively approached, can provide the inspiration so important to a children's writer. Therefore, know them for what they are, little monsters, adorable rascals, angels with dirty faces or troublesome teens, call them what you will but honestly get to know them if you wish to avoid the many pitfalls that await the writer for children.

If you have read thus far and have now decided upon the age group for which you wish to write, then the next step is market research. Buy anything and everything produced for either tots, tweens, teens or young adults and read, read, read. See the strength with which the characters are formed, how the plots are evolved and the authenticity of the background. Remember, to get it in print, you must get it right.

3
ANALYSING THE MARKET

Better ask twice than lose your way once
Danish Proverb

Having established a degree of understanding with your reader, it is now important to study the sort of material bought by editors and publishers. This is done by market research and many publishers will supply on request (and a sae) a list of their requirements or guidelines. It is false, however, to assume that whatever style and content appeared in last week's periodicals will continue to be acceptable to the editor over any long period of time. It is, therefore, a mistake to attempt to do your market research using publications that are several years, or even months, old as styles change so rapidly.

EDITORIAL GUIDELINES

Editorial guidelines should be regarded as a set of rules which applies specifically to their publishing house. They will list their various publications or series, giving detailed information of their various requirements.

House style is important, together with the length of manuscript, content and format and whether or not you will be required to provide illustrations. Generally speaking, publishers require similar presentation, but it is as well to check before submitting your work that the publishing house of your choice has no individual peculiarities.

Perhaps the most important factor contained within the guidelines of a publishing house is that of length. It is wrong to assume that you can simply write an article, a short story or a book to what may appear to be its natural length and expect it to be acceptable to an editor who has carefully planned the pagination of his publication to allow for a specific amount of space to be occupied by a specific team.

A short story in a magazine or comic, for example, would probably run to between 1,200 and 1,400 words if it is to occupy a single page and allow for an illustration of moderate size. Submit a manuscript of 2,000 words and, no matter how good the plot or quality of your work, it will undoubtedly be rejected. A busy editor has no time to sub-edit or rewrite your manuscript. Remember, too, that to disregard such a requirement is the hallmark of the amateur or novice writer.

It is difficult, if not impossible, for a novice to write exactly to the required length and in order that the editorial guidelines do not create a mental straitjacket, begin by writing your story to its natural length, for it is then that the tale will be well told. If, however, it becomes necessary for you to trim it to size, then you will be able to go back and prune away the dead wood, the unnecessary line of dialogue, the description that is too lengthy, or even (in most extreme cases) to completely dispense with a secondary character. Long passages of purple prose or description upon which, at the time, you congratulated yourself may, in the final cull, be the very pieces which will have to go.

Should the manuscript fall short of the editorial requirement then, once again, read your draft with great care. How well have you drawn your characters? Can they be improved upon by showing a little more detail relevant to the story but against an additional background? Have you included enough dialogue and most important of all, have you put onto paper the story that was in your mind? Too often, we assume that the reader is in possession of facts that the writer knows comprise an important part of the story when, in fact, they are still locked within the writer's mind. If your story needs expansion, then you may have room to introduce an additional character, a sub-plot or to improve upon your characterisation or passages of description.

In order to avoid confusion, it is my intention to explore

first one market area and then another, covering material both fact and fiction first for the pre-school child and then each age group in turn.

PRE AND PRIMARY SCHOOL MARKETS

It has been my experience that one of the best nursery grounds for the would-be writer for the very young child is within the range of comics produced by D.C. Thomson. But before you consider writing for this market you must understand that it is by no means as simple as it looks.

A look along your newsagent's shelves will reveal that there are several other publishing houses catering for this age group, so select half a dozen comics from a number of publishing houses catering for the read aloud pre-school age group and read them from cover to cover, not once but many times before doing an analysis of what they contain.

You will soon realise that the pages between the covers of the pre-school comic are peopled by anthropomorphised animals, toys, witches, wizards and pleasant little visitors from outer space. Even in today's high-tech world, a sprinkling of wee folk, fairies, elves and sprites have still managed to survive.

Books for this age group range from a variety of educational subjects such as the old standby *A is for Apple, B is for Ball* picture books to clearly illustrated guides to colours, numbers and animals found in both woodland and zoos. In each case, the child is encouraged to identify what it sees in picture form under the direction of an adult, thereby widening its vocabulary and comprehension.

A rapid expansion of the child's scope for learning becomes apparent during the first few months of primary school education. New disciplines must be incorporated into its day, new friendships forged and the learning process becomes a serious undertaking.

Comics for this age group begin, during the next two years of the child's life, to mature in their content, offering a more stimulating mixture, often incorporating craft articles, quizzes and competitions alongside slapstick humour and adventure featuring children of a similar age to that of the reader.

Non-fiction books for this age group cover such subjects as, for example, life on a farm showing a day in the life of a farm worker or perhaps a simple explanation in captioned pictures of how a car is made from one end of the assembly line to the other.

On the fiction side, the child is encouraged to improve its reading ability by a wide range of large print, well illustrated story books. The tales themselves still have their roots in the unspoiled magic which exists within the mind of the very young child, which once again includes witches, wizards, aliens, adventure and humour.

By the time the child progresses to the junior school at the age of seven, his reading ability has improved, and once again the world of comics and juvenile magazines caters for his rapidly maturing taste.

The slapstick element is increased with little or no regard for the intrusion of reality. A few specialist magazines catering for new found hobbies may well, due to demand, appear on the newsagent's bill at the end of the month.

Suitably encouraged, the child will take on a new interest in the book world, for it is now that he can curl up with a volume of his own choice from a library or bookshop and read to his heart's content.

The wide range of 'read alone' books which have appeared in recent years cover both fact and fiction and are invaluable to the developing mind. Within this age range, too, you will find a growing trend towards series books. A 'series' book can best be described as a book written specifically for inclusion in a list of titles of a similar length and general format.

Hamish Hamilton, for example, produce the *Gazelle* series, which are promoted as: 'A series of lively and enjoyable stories which are ideal for children who have just started to read by themselves. Each story, with its clear, large type is simple but complete and will be invaluable in helping children to move from picture to story books.'

Antelope, from the same publisher, set out to be: 'A series of imaginative and exciting stories especially written by popular authors for children who have just begun to enjoy reading complete books on their own.' Printed in large, clear type and with a wide variety of themes and settings, they are geared to today's children and demonstrate the pleasure to be gained from reading.

Cartwheels, also by Hamish Hamilton, describe themselves as: 'A bright colourful series of easy reader books with a simple vocabulary and with lively illustrations on each page. The series, containing a wide variety of stories to suit all young tastes, is ideal for children who are just starting to read by themselves'.

The *Read Alone* series from Viking, again in large print with black and white line drawings, claim to be: 'An entertaining series specifically designed for all new readers who want to start reading a whole book on their own.'

Penguin Books are the publishers of the *Kites* series, again intended for beginner readers, describing themselves as: 'A series of lively and interesting stories guaranteed to encourage the new reader.'

If you feel this particular age group is one you can identify with, and for whom you have decided to write, then clearly the message is to read as many of these books as you can. Then be sure to tailor your manuscript to fit into one or another of the series before offering it to a publisher.

Should your mind be set on writing non-fiction, based perhaps upon your own knowledge of a subject, then this age group can be counted upon to be among the most eager to explore new areas of knowledge. Puffin Books, published by the Penguin Group, offer a wide range of titles in the *Young Puffin Factbook* series, covering such areas as personal safety and health coupled with detailed but easy to understand books on how modern technology such as radio, television and computers work. Many of these find their way into the eager hands of teachers, who are engaged with their young students upon a class project.

OLDER READERS

As young readers approach their tenth or eleventh birthday,

their reading tastes mature dramatically and, once again, the world of comics and juvenile publications is there to answer their need. Whilst continuing to include humour, boys' comics will now include stories set against a background of sport, science fiction or adventure. The girls' publications, on the other hand, incorporate as their setting the world of horse riding, ballet, sports, fashion and school life. Whilst a mixture of settings such as these may be found in individual stories within the pages of a single juvenile magazine, the book world, understandably, is more specific.

The same background material is, nonetheless, relevant to this age group. Bantam Books, with their worldwide distribution, cater well for this age group. *The Saddle Club* is a series of adventure stories with an equine background guaranteed to rivet the attention of any horse loving teenager, while a gentle entry into the world of teenage romance is the *Sweet Valley Twins* series from the same publishers. The wide range of titles in the Choose Your Own Adventure style found its most eager readers in this age group. The books were, from the parental viewpoint, an excellent buy, allowing as they did the good value of many stories for the price of one. The format employed was that the author placed the reader in the position of the central character, allowing him or her to make a personal choice of action at each twist in the tale, each chosen route providing a new storyline and a different ending. The basic background to each book was one of science fiction, crime detection or history and provided the young reader with hours of entertainment, an exciting concept for writers and readers alike and one which will be explored more fully later.

By thirteen or fourteen, the young reader often makes the leap from junior to adult fiction. In recent years this age group has become well catered for in both the world of comics and books.

All sporting activities, teenage fashion and the world of pop music are adequately covered and coupled with pertinent storylines, produce a variety of magazines which have an increasingly enthusiastic following. Whilst the book world, acknowledging its readers' needs to tackle the realities of life, caters for that need with a range of excellent material.

Puffin Plus, an imprint of Puffin Books, deals well with such subjects as war, racial issues, sex, drugs, divorce, stepparents, abuse and bullying. These books involve the reader throughout, helping him come to terms with the many insecurities experienced by every child who suffers the agonies of the transition from teens to adult.

With the recent change in the law regarding children's rights, a whole new area is open to exploration by the writer of teenage fiction. At last, children have a legal right to be heard in such matters as parental access following a divorce. Many children whose lives have been disrupted by the regular, and at times unwelcome, periods they have been forced by law to spend first with one parent and then another are now open to examination by the courts. For the first time, the child's own emotional requirements may now be taken into account.

Whilst on the one hand, this may solve the problems for many an unhappy child, it would also place power in the hands of the young and inexperienced which may well lead to unforeseen difficulties.

This change in the law will not, you can be sure, be overlooked by writers for this age group who, through their own research and skill, will be in a position to educate and inform those young readers who may find themselves involved in a legal and emotional situation.

KEEP A NOTEBOOK

Begin your market research by buying a good quality, hardbacked notebook indexed at the side for easy reference. The information you commit to its pages will be of use to you for many years to come and if you are ever stuck for a market, leaf through its pages.

Start with your analysis of the publications you have chosen for market research. The title of the publication (or in the case of a book, the publisher) together with the publisher's full name and address should appear at the top of the page. Then should come a list of its contents, noting at the side of each item whether it is a text story, (that is to say, one with little or no illustration) a picture-strip story (one that is told in an illustrated form with either captions beneath each picture or word bubbles) and whether there are any general interest items, craft articles or poems. Make a note of the approximate length of each of these. It will be necessary to update the information from time to time as old titles, ideas and characters are dropped and new characters and trends emerge.

Where books are concerned, the page should have the content of the material accepted by the publishing house and an outline of the requirements for each series of books, together with their approximate length and full scope of subject material.

When embarking upon market research, it is inevitable that, at the back of the mind of the writer will be the desire to discover a market suitable for targeting with his own specialist ideas. In the majority of cases, it would be true to say that we enjoy writing that which we most enjoy reading. An adult devotee of the macabre will, in all possibility, produce an excellent spine-chiller for the teenage market.

A lover of historical adventure will almost certainly be capable of writing something within the same time zone for younger readers. An addict of science fiction or fantasy will find themselves well equipped to produce a manuscript on similar lines for the next generation.

It therefore makes good sense to shortlist those publishers whose lists regularly include similar work to your chosen genre. Reference to the *Writers' & Artists' Yearbook* will make quite clear which publishing houses deal solely in non-fiction or a mix of the two. It will clearly explain which of these houses deals with publications for children, and the nature of those publications.

Once you have shortlisted a selection of publishing houses, send for their guidelines but do not rely on these alone. Your librarian will supply you with examples from each list which you would be well advised to study for style and format before submitting your own manuscript.

NON-FICTION AND THE MAGAZINE MARKET

Non-fiction items of interest to specific age groups can often be successfully introduced to a magazine editor by either letter or telephone. Contrary to belief editors are approachable and, although they may not always have the time to hold lengthy conversations, they are usually willing to discover an idea for an article, or indeed a series of articles on a given subject.

Remember that to a growing child, the beginning of each new day is another step in their voyage of discovery, the discovery of what are, to you the adult, well known facts.

A few years ago, I had in my charge an intelligent three year old boy. As we wandered through the local park, he pounced on a leaf blown onto the path by the autumn breeze. For a few moments, he examined its texture, colour and veined structure. At last, he directed a puzzled frown in my direction.

'Why is a leaf?' he asked.

It took me several minutes and some carefully phrased questions to discover that his limited vocabulary was proving a stumbling block. In the hope that I would hit on the right answer, I sat with him on a bench beneath a huge oak and explained, at length, the life story of the tree from acorn to its present magnificent height. I thought I deserved a round of applause but having, I now realise, satisfied his curiosity within the first thirty seconds of my diatribe, I had to be content with a dismissive nod of understanding and a plea for an ice cream at the nearby kiosk.

That day, despite his fidgeting, my young charge learned the life-cycle of an oak tree and I learned that, as the attention span of a three year old is less than a minute, over-explanation effectively kills enthusiasm and interest. Nonetheless, the life cycle of that tree could well have formed the basis of a non-fiction book for the early reader.

Although the world of comics will be covered in greater detail in a later chapter, it is nonetheless worth mentioning at this point that a good editor will always be prepared to consider the inclusion of a new character within the pages of the publication he governs. It will, of course, need to be in keeping with the current storylines but perhaps offer mileage in the form of a new and exciting central character. Study the publication very carefully before submitting any idea of this nature and offer it to the editor in the form of one complete manuscript, together with a synopsis of further storylines for the character, for his consideration. If the concept meets with his approval, you may well have the pleasure of seeing the character you originated appearing week after week.

Many magazines aimed at the adult market often carry a page for children. Women's magazines in particular will feature a short read aloud story, a regular three to four frame strip story, poems, craft articles and filler-length informative snippets on nature or general knowledge subjects.

MAKING A MARKET

In some cases the children's feature is written by a member of the magazine staff, others may be the work of an established freelance. Often however there are openings for newcomers: for example, several print a children's story of between five and eight hundred words. As with every market, however, it is limited – but do not despair: if you have tried these established markets without success, go out and make a new one for yourself.

If you, or a member of your family have a specialist knowledge or an interesting hobby, you probably take an adult magazine which caters for it. Does it have a children's page? Ask yourself if not, why not? It may, of course, be that the subject is not suitable. On the other hand, it may be that the idea of a column or a page for children has not been presented with sufficient conviction to the editor. Children develop a surprisingly early interest in adult hobbies, for example needlework, knitting, fishing, collecting, car mechanics, electronics and music, the range is limitless.

Breaking into a new market is not impossible but if you are to interest the editor sufficiently for him to set aside valuable space in his otherwise adult periodical, you must convince him at the outset that you are capable of increasing his readership successfully by casting your net into the pool of the next generation. You must also show that you can sustain their loyalty to his magazine by maintaining their interest over a long period, and that you are prepared to guarantee that a regular, trouble-free manuscript will arrive on his desk in time for each weekly or monthly deadline. It is, therefore, pointless to approach any adult magazine with a short, one-off idea for children.

Many years ago, I suggested to the editor of a local newspaper a new idea for inclusion on a page I had been writing for several years. Children, I pointed out, were born collectors and my postbag had often contained letters telling me all about the young correspondent, their family and friends, school life and hobbies. A high percentage, I had noticed, collected something: pencils, rubbers, fans, models, football programmes and much, much more.

I proposed a visit, with the parents' permission, to interview each child who would then appear in a new feature entitled *Collector's Corner*. With editorial approval, the first feature went to press and I was, over the following three years, deluged with young collectors who yearned to see details of themselves and their collections in print.

The child's story of how the collection began and how many items it currently boasted appeared alongside their photograph. Only the child's name and the area in which he or she lived was published and contact with the collector was invited through my own address. Many letters were passed on to each child in this manner, the letter re-addressed to the parent in each case. In my opinion the effort and postal charges were a small price to pay to maintain the comparative anonymity and safety of a vulnerable child in the world of today.

The same degree of anonymity was observed when, upon realising there were several national collectors' magazines which did not support a children's page, I successfully approached an editor with the idea of the *Squirrel Club*. Following the first few articles, I was once again faced with a bulging postbag and another regular children's column was established in an otherwise adult magazine.

Ask any teacher or, preferably, any child and you will discover a range of interests for which you can supply material drawn either from your own knowledge or from your own research.

A gardening magazine may take a *Polly's Plot* feature. Remember how exciting it was to see a bean sandwiched between wet blotting paper and the side of the jam jar as it began to put out roots and shoots? Or to marvel at the speed with which the mustard and cress grew in a tray on the kitchen window sill? Whilst the world in which the child of today functions has, in the last twenty years, changed beyond all recognition, children have not altered. Generation after generation, they still love to see things grow.

A series of craft articles, again relevant to the magazine's specialist interest, may well be acceptable to the editor. Pictures from pressed flowers, decorated plant pots or tree bark sculpture, particularly if illustrated with drawings or photographs, could well prove acceptable to the editor of that same gardening magazine.

The fact that the world of the child has widened in recent years to incorporate many hi-tech scientific advances means that the world of the writer, too, has room for expansion.

The simplified explanation of the construction and use of a micro-chip, for example, is equally satisfying to that of watching the growth of the bean in the jam jar to a generation of children whose technical knowledge outstrips that of their parents.

If, therefore, you feel you have sufficient technical knowledge in one or other area of science, then by all means use that knowledge, coupled with the skills of writing for children, to assist in their education.

Do not, however, discount the importance of the range of games and hobbies enjoyed by earlier generations. The revival of many of these ideas has led not only to hundreds of successful articles but to a range of toys based on the simple experiments familiar to the parental generation. The mysterious behaviour of iron filings in the presence of a magnet, the toy model boat chugging happily on the surface of water, powered by nothing more than bicarbonate of soda still fascinates.

Whether, therefore, you have the knowledge to incorporate new technology or old ideas into your writing, at the end of the day it is the way they are presented which will determine whether they are acceptable to an editor.

Fiction is harder to place than fact, although a short story for an age group governed by the subject matter of the magazine is not outside the realms of acceptance if it is relevant to the readership. Watch for new magazines on the newsstand; if they lack a page for children, write a suitable story or article and submit it to the editor with a polite letter and return postage. If he likes the idea, you could find yourself writing for him on a regular basis.

Never say, 'There is no market for my work.' Go out and make one.

4
VOCABULARY

A child, when it begins to speak,
learns what it is that it knows.

John Hall Wheelock

The first sounds made by a child range, according to its mood, from a contented gurgle to an earsplitting yell. Astonishingly, mothers are able to understand (or at worst guess with a surprising degree of accuracy, fortunate for the child) just what it is their little bundle of joy is trying to communicate.

First words are greeted rapturously, the wily little mite appearing to curry favour with one or other parent by triumphantly pronouncing a barely recognisable Mama or Dada.

The next two or three years are painstakingly spent in parent/infant speech tuition until, by the time the little darling is around four years of age, Mum and Dad have begun to wish he or she had been born with an on/off switch.

EXPLORING THE RANGE

Within those first four or five years of a child's life, it acquires, we are told by the experts, a working knowledge of around 2,000 words. The youngster is, however, capable of using only a selection of one, two or three syllable words, amounting to approximately 600 to 700 at most. It is within this limited area of comprehension and vocabulary that you, the writer, must work if a story for the pre-school age group is to be understood by the child, or indeed, purchased by an editor.

Read as much material as possible for this age group and listen carefully to the way a parent painstakingly explains something to their offspring. Gradually, you will begin to appreciate the simple, colourful words with which you must communicate.

When young children begin to read, they neither want nor need long descriptive passages. You can forget about, *The song of the birds floated up into the blue sky, where pink-tinged clouds heralded the break of day.* Just say, *It was morning.*

Avoid: *The tiring journey past the post office and the butchers, round the corner, across the park, around the back of the supermarket, until at last they came...*

It was a long way to Grandma's house is more to the point and will better hold the attention of the very young listener.

The writer, however, should continually bear in mind the edge-blurring factor when attempting to outline the reading ability of specific age groups. It is usual for children to have begun the process of learning to read by the age of six. Individual ability thereafter determines the speed of progress. Interest areas, humour appreciation and the use of vocabulary, however, have broadened considerably. For the six to eight year old child, who can still legitimately ask for a story to be read aloud, this wider comprehension allows entry into a whole new world of adventure.

Throughout the ages, the continuing appeal of pictures to the young child is undeniable. Parents, using the most simple form of picture strip story will actively encourage the pre-school child to read and increase its vocabulary. The young listeners become totally involved in the stories as they eagerly point out the illustrated characters and situations relevant to the text. Later, left alone with the same comics, the young readers will identify the written word by using the pictures to help them through the story.

Initially, when writing for children, many authors find it hard to make the distinction between what is and what is not comprehensible to the young reader. A method of assessment which can be of invaluable help to the novice writer is the Fog Index Formula, developed by Robert Gunning. This is an equation which, when applied to a piece of work, signifies the approximate age and intelligence group who will best appreciate the content.

The formula was devised after detailed research work on the readability of writing styles. Gunning and his team singled out the factors considered to have the most bearing on reading difficulty. His research led him to devise an equation based on the average sentence length contained within a 100 word passage, taking into account such factors as the number of three or more syllable words, proper names and so forth. Once calculated, he combined the average number of words per sentence with the school grade level of the reader, to produce the Fog Index equation set out below:

Gunning suggests that you:

Jot down the number of words in successive sentences. You may wish to take several samples of 100 words, spaced evenly through it, stopping the sentence count with the sentence which ends nearest the 100 word total. By dividing the total number of words in the passage by the number of sentences you will arrive at the average sentence length of the passage.

Next, count the number of words of three syllables or more in your selected 100 word passage. Do not count proper names, combinations of short easy words, like *shop-keeper* and verb forms which are made three syllable by adding *ed* or *es*. You now have the percentage of hard words in the passage.

To arrive at the Fog Index, total the two foregoing factors and multiply by 0.4.

To better illustrate the point, I have chosen two passages from my own published work. For the first, I have taken an extract from an *Elfie* story written for the under sixes: the second illustrates the dialogue between two characters in frames 1–4 of a picture strip story for young teenage girls.

1. Extract from D.C. Thomson's *Twinkle* Comic's *Elfie*:
Elfie, the tiny elf, lives secretly in Mary's dolls house. When he makes things happen, Mary thinks it is magic! Elfie's best friend is Mary's dog, Poochie.

1. Little Elfie was very sad. Poochie and Mary were going away on holiday and leaving him behind.

2. Poor Elfie felt lonely. He wandered into the garden, where he met his friend, Peter Pigeon and told him what was wrong.

3. 'Don't worry,' cooed his birdie chum, 'Climb on my back and I will take you to the beach. You can have a holiday too!'

4. Soon, they were at the seaside. 'Look, there's somewhere for you to stay!' cried Peter, pointing with his wing. 'A sand castle!'

Gunning Fog Index Equation:

113 words: 13 sentences: 4 long words

Fog Index Factor 0.4

$^{113}/_{13} = 8.7$ (words per sentence)

$^{4}/_{113} \times 100 = 3.5$ (% long words to total)

$8.7 + 3.5 = 12.2 \times 0.4 = 4.88$ Fog Index

2. Extract from IPC's *Girls*

L: But why? I was only five when Mum and Dad were killed – I've never even met him.

HM: I know Lorna – but he is your legal guardian.

HM: He's always written regularly to you and taken a keen interest in your progress here.

L: I still don't want to go, Miss Forsyth.

L: Please can't you ask him to let me stay here?

HM: I'm sorry my dear, but there is nothing I can do about it.

HM: I can understand your apprehension at such a change, but once you're settled in, I'm sure you will be happy in your new life.

Gunning Fog Index Equation:

96 words: 7 sentences: 5 long words

Fog Index Factor 0.4

$^{96}/_{7} = 13.7$ (words per sentence)

$^{5}/_{96} \times 100 = 5.2$ (% long words to total)

$13.7 = 5.2 = 18.9 \times 0.4 = 7.56$ Fog Index

By applying the Gunning Fog Index, you will see that the resulting reading age is between four and five for the first passage, whilst for the second passage it is between seven and eight. Whilst the Fog Index is helpful in gauging the reader age level of your work, its usefulness is as a guide only. It would be stifling to your creativity to work strictly to this complicated formula.

However, I have devised my own simplified equation, based on Gunning, which I have found an invaluable aid to pitching my work and the correct age levels of the various strip writing markets. The figures are basically the same but because dialogue and, therefore, proper names are used extensively in this medium, I include these words in my calculations to read as follows:

1. Select a passage of one hundred words and count the number of sentences it contains.

2. Divide the number of sentences into one hundred, giving you the average number of words in a sentence.

3. Count the number of words with three syllables or more.

4. Add this figure to the average number.

5. Multiply the total by four and divide by ten.

Therefore, the equation for Example 1 would read:

100 (words) divided by 13 (sentences) = 7 + 4 (words with three or more syllables) = 11 × 4 = 44 divided by 10 = 4 approx.

And for Example 2, the equation would read:

100 (words) divided by 7 (sentences) = 12 + 5 (words with three or more syllables) = 17 × 4 = 68 divided by 10 = 7 approx.

The final figure has nothing to do with an exact reader age but if you take the time to apply the exercise to a range of publications for all ages, you will have the satisfaction of seeing a definite scale emerge. Using a similar method on your own manuscript will establish the suitability for the age group at which it is aimed.

The use of a suitable vocabulary is, on the part of the writer, a matter of common-sense but one should remember that young children are constantly embracing new concepts and widening their powers of expression. Offer the child some new words, adequately explained, and you will assist his education and his appreciation of the world in which he lives – but bear in mind words which are difficult to pronounce can temporarily defeat the child that has just begun to learn to read. For example, words of foreign origin, unless absolutely essential to your tale, should be avoided. However, one of your characters may be from another country and although the vocabulary will be spoken largely in English, a well-explained word in a native tongue could become part of the characterisation. For example:

The little doll began to sob.
'What's the matter?' asked the teddy bear, 'are you still unhappy?'
'Oui,' she nodded, 'I miss my mama.'

Puns are fun to the adult mind but the subtlety of their humour is lost on the under six year olds. Puns, defined as 'a quibble', 'play upon words' or 'witticism and parodies, which are best explained as caricatures or ludicrous imitations', can only be appreciated by the older reader at a later stage, once the basic art of fluent reading has been accomplished. Once this plateau of subconscious reading has been attained and the child no longer stumbles over new words, it is then left free to fully appreciate the subtleties of gradually maturing humour.

THE USE OF SLANG

Although slang begins to creep into the child's vocabulary from its first day at school and its use, from the writer's point of view, can add realism to a story, it should be used with caution. Remember that what is in fashion one moment is out the next. Not only does it serve to date your work, but few parents in the read-aloud age group would approve of the use of slang. Market research will, however, reveal that it is constantly used in its topical form in the great majority of comics and juvenile magazines suitable for readers of nine and over.

Despite the snatches of children's conversation I regularly overhear through my open window as they make their way home from a nearby school, as a writer, I must continue to believe that pre-school children do not cuss. If one of the characters in your story stubs his toe, whether it is bruised or broken, you as the writer will allow him only to utter a mild *oh bother!* or *ouch!*

The slang used by children changes rapidly. When writing a contemporary story destined for a comparatively short life between the pages of a comic, slang must therefore be relevant to the setting in which your characters function.

Children of all ages evolve their own language which, in many cases, is inexplicable to the adult mind. For example, to denote their approval words like *bad* or *wicked* have recently come to the fore. While *brill*, *mega* and *heavy* have been used to denote the same level of approval. Rejection or dislike has, however, been expressed by use of words like *naff* and *gross*.

When writing a book, which will hopefully enjoy a far longer life than a comic, slang rarely appears. When it does it is consciously used skilfully to illustrate the action, timespan and location of the story. Some of the expressions in these snatches of dialogue within an extract from Percival Christopher Wren's *Beau Geste*, for example, would never be heard today but perfectly convey the historical setting and relationship between the characters.

> ... 'It can't be true,' I said, 'It's impossible.'
>
> 'Of course it is, fat-head,' replied Digby, 'he's off on the romantic tack...'
>
> ... 'Don't be a colossal ass,' interrupted Digby...'
>
> ... 'I am not asking you to tell Aunt, or the police, am I bun-head?'...

For the more advanced reader, the characters in the stories you write will often include people from other cultures and lands. Once again, there is no need to beat your reader over the head with the over-use of phonetically written dialogue to convince them of your character's roots. As with the little French doll, the occasional telltale word or phrase should be enough to paint the necessary picture in the mind of the reader.

In *The Fib And Other Stories* by George Layton, the north

of England setting comes over loud and clear in the dialogue of the characters:

> ... I told him that was nothing because Miss Taylor had given everybody in our class sixpence but he didn't believe me.
> 'Gerraway, you bloomin' fibber.'
> 'She did, didn't she Tony?'
> Tony shook his head.
> 'Did she heckers like – she wouldn't give 'owt away'...

The page in its entirety contains only these few words of dialect, yet they are more than sufficient to convey the feel, time and place of the story.

DIALOGUE

Realistic dialogue is the hidden strength in every story, whether for young or old. Properly used, it will create and strengthen the character, while at the same time, moving the story along.

An example of the way dialogue and vocabulary reinforce characterisation is shown in the following extract from *Final Curtain*, a book of short ghost stories I wrote for young teens. The story, entitled *Return Journey* is centred around children living in a country area having to use the school bus:

> Jason Green panted to a halt, just in time to see the school bus disappear into the distance.
> 'Oh crikey, not again,' he groaned, clutching at the painful stitch in his side. 'That's the second time this week I've missed it. Old Wilson will be hopping mad if I turn up late.'

From the moment Jason speaks, his age is easy to determine. It is clear, too, that he is reasonably well-mannered and worried about his situation.

Vocabulary is equally important when determining the pace of a story. Long words have the effect of slowing down the speed of a passage, while short, staccato phrases will quicken the pace. In this further extract from *Return Journey*, the bus hurtles towards disaster:

> They had just reached the summit of the hill that led down to the bridge over the river and the village beyond, when the bus slewed on the ice and began to slide, wheel-locked, down the steep gradient. Jenny began to scream as the sides of the vehicle scraped showers of snow from the roadside bushes, mercifully blanketing her vision. Carson fought to regain control, sobbing with fear as the bridge over the river loomed nearer and nearer. Horror numbed Jason's mind as he closed his eyes and prayed hard, which was why he could not explain later how one moment Carson was at the wheel and the next, grovelling alongside him, cowering on his knees in the aisle.
>
> In his place at the wheel sat Mr Barnes, his shoulders hunched as he struggled to bring the bus under control. At the last possible moment, Jason felt the wheels grip the icy surface and he saw the elderly driver swing the bus sharply to the right. He heard the screech of stone on metal as the vehicle clipped the grey parapet and plunged to a halt, ankle-deep in snow in River Meadow, only yards from the water's edge.

By keeping the sentences relatively short and using emotive words such as *slewed*, *wheel-locked*, *scream* and *loomed*, it is possible to convey the feeling of the bus sliding downhill into danger. By closing the character's eyes and suspending him briefly in terror-filled seconds, further unnecessary and lengthy description is avoided. As the tension builds and danger is mercifully averted, the passage is brought to an abrupt halt, giving a feeling of breathless relief.

HUMOUR

One method guaranteed to release tension is the use of humour. When considering humour in writing for children,

57

the first and most important thing to understand is that their level of appreciation of humour is not the same as an adult's.

The success of adult humour has its roots in topicality, satire, politics, adult relationships and sex. Many of these areas are outside the comprehension of the growing child, who will best be made to laugh by anything that contains an element of slapstick, the downfall of authority or an element of the often harmless, downright smutty.

The first of these, slapstick, is almost totally confined to the wide range of comics for readers across the age groups. *The Beano* and *Dandy* have survived several generations of *Dennis the Menace* and *The Bash Street Kids*, their characters still continuing to slip on banana skins, clout one another with outsize clubs, smash priceless antiques and become the recipients of custard pies.

The challenge and ultimate triumph over authority represented by parents and teachers is a reliable backbone of humour for the young reader, and once again comics play an important part. By representing the authoritative figure in an identifiable form, the young reader can unwittingly play out his or her fantasy, enjoying triumph in an otherwise impossible manner. The life of a child is necessarily governed by such areas of authority against which they have little or no defence. Again, you should remember that the range of a child's emotions is the same as an adult, only the vocabulary with which to express it is lacking.

In this particular circumstance, it is not so much the lack of vocabulary but the inadvisability of using it that prevents the child from voicing what is often just a viewpoint.

Humour in books requires a greater degree of subtlety. With the exception of books for the very young, the text must rely upon its own strength unaided by pictures. In my own recently published book *Snortyblog Comes to Earth*, a class of primary school children are delighted when a particularly unpleasant teacher is dealt with in an unusual but effective way:

'Tisn't fair,' Snorty felt his ears begin to glow red. His new friends might have been wrong in reaching their classroom later than the other children but it was partly his fault and Miss Naylor really seemed to enjoy being unkind. He had to do something to help Sarah and Jay before things got any worse.

'I'll Blogbozzle her, that's what I'll do,' he muttered and before Jay could stop him, Snorty wriggled out of his pocket and scrambled onto the boy's shoulder, swivelled his ears to point directly at the back of the teacher's head. Then, closing his eyes, he Blogbeamed as hard as he could in her direction. A blue spark bounced through the air and settled just behind Miss Naylor's left ear.

At first, nothing seemed to happen but as soon as the teacher began to speak, it was obvious that the Blogbeam had done its work.

'Won nerdlihc ew lliw teg no htiw eht nossel.'

At first, the children stared at their teacher in silence.

'What did she say?' whispered Sarah.

Jay shrugged, 'Sounded like double Dutch to me.'

Miss Naylor, who looked a little puzzled, straightened her thin shoulders and tried again, 'Ekat tuo ruoy skoob.'

One of the children giggled nervously.

'On gnihgual!' shouted the now seriously worried teacher.

'Please, Miss, are you all right?' asked Jennifer who, as everybody knew, wanted to be a nurse when she grew up and was always looking for an excuse to practice her first aid, 'Would you like a drink of water?'

Miss Naylor certainly looked as if she needed something. Her face had turned quite red and she kept opening her mouth and then shutting it again, as if she was afraid of what might come out.

'On knaht uoy,' she squeaked, her hand flying to her mouth. 'Ho raed.'

By now, the children were laughing out loud, 'Oh Miss, you are funny,' gasped Jay's friend, Paul, holding his sides, tears running down his cheeks, 'Do it again, oh please, do it again.'

'Pots ti! Pots ti!' sobbed the frightened teacher and rushed from the classroom, slamming the door behind her.

The children all started to talk at once.

'What's up with old Nasty?'

'She was talking scribble like my baby brother.'

'No, it was Russian, I bet you.'

'I'm sure she's not well,' said Jennifer but Jay knew better.

'She was talking backwards, that's what it was,' he said, 'And it was something you did, I saw you,' he accused Snorty, who was safely back in Jay's blazer pocket and happily humming to himself.

The past master of this technique whose work has been loved by young readers for many years is, of course, Roald Dahl who, upon his own admission, enjoyed debunking teachers and similar authority figures.

The message is loud and clear. Authors may deal with a transgressing adult character as harshly or humorously as they wish, but the writer must be wary in the treatment of a transgressing child.

A spoilt brat, a bully or a sneak should receive their come-uppance from their peers. Children have an innate sense of justice and it will better satisfy the reader if a sharp lesson is delivered by themselves rather than by the authoritative figure of the adult.

Downright smutty humour is once again employed to great effect by Roald Dahl but perhaps the prime example of 'behind the bike shed' lavatory humour came to the fore with Raymond Briggs' *Fungus the Bogeyman*.

References to *snot*, *sick* and *slime* might turn the adult stomach but can be guarantee to evoke a snigger from the young reader. If you have read the book, you may wonder why it should have achieved such a following or indeed, how it appeared acceptable to Hamish Hamilton, its publisher. To the experienced editorial eye, however, it is clear that the writer has the essential ability to inhabit the somewhat grubby mind of the child, thereby establishing an instant rapport with the reader. Part of this appreciation factor could well be the delight felt by the child at the reaction of its parents to something so outrageously naughty.

By the time the child reaches the eleven plus age group, it has become a competent reader, with a wide appreciation of the world at large. During this period of growth many readers pole-vault into the world of adult literature, but the age group is well catered for with what is known as Young Adult novels covering such areas essential to the teenager as, for example, coming to terms with emotional upheaval. Many of today's children are forced to face such realities as parents divorcing, the relocation of the family involving a break in the continuity of their life and more importantly, the loss of their circle of friends, terminal illness, sex and unwanted pregnancies, the lack of parental understanding and peer disapproval.

It needs a delicate hand on the part of the writer to cope with the ugly realisms of life, and once again it is essential to get to know your reader. You must learn to use vocabulary which, when employed in the written word, will deliver your story on an acceptable level.

To immerse yourself, therefore, in a vocabulary comprehensible to the child at various stages of its educational growth is one of the cornerstones of writing for children. I would urge the would-be writer to acquire anything and everything currently written for children and read, read, read.

5
CHARACTERISATION

*I present myself to you in a form suitable
to the relationship I wish to achieve with you.*
Luigi Pirandello *The Pleasure of Honesty*

Before looking at characterisation, the first step in the construction of a read aloud story, a word of warning: never allow the lack of a title to delay the writing of the story. On occasions, your character will, as you develop him or her, suggest its own title: the plot itself may similarly prove to be an inspiration. If, however, you find it imperative to put something at the top of your page before you can begin, use your first thoughts only as a working title. More often than not something far better will emerge during the writing of the story itself, perhaps a descriptive phrase or a comment by one of the characters will say it all. Titles can prove an important factor in the acceptance of your work, if only by catching the editor's eye. Do not, however, break your heart if he feels he knows better than you, the author. A lot of valuable time can be wasted looking for the right title, only to have it dismissed and replaced by something which often may seem, in your view, inappropriate or by no means as catchy.

On one occasion, despite suggesting what I considered to be an inspired and emotive title, it was obviously not suitable to the editor and *Crushaloop*, the amiable python became *Loopy Lulu*. Disappointingly, I was not aware of the change until both story and altered title appeared in print.

If your title should happen to be used, it could be for one of many reasons: perhaps it was just relevant to the story, perhaps it was humorous, but above all perhaps it happened to intrigue the editor.

CHARACTERS

Whether the first wisp of story idea presents itself to you in plot form or as a character is unimportant, provided you write it down immediately. Characters, once discovered, usually suggest their own plots and certainly the problems that they would logically encounter. For all age groups your characters must be recognisable as good or bad, enabling the reader to establish their sympathies at the outset.

Keep a notebook containing a list of likely types and add to it constantly. Rule its pages into two columns, heading them *Name & Character* and *Type*. In the first, allowing five or six lines between each entry, list your characters. These may be drawn from the real or imaginative world which both you and your young reader inhabit. Every item around you can, for the sake of a children's story, become animated – but before you include it in your list, consider whether or not it 'says' something to you, whether you can work with it or whether it lacks the necessary inspiration.

Will the chair in which you sit come immediately to life in your imagination as shabby and sad, or new and proud? These are the thoughts which should be entered under *Type* in column two. Will it resent being sat upon, or will it perhaps prove to be a special magic dreaming chair for anyone who falls asleep against its cushions? What about that china figure on the shelf? Is it chipped? If so, how did the accident occur and how would it feel about the damage once you have given it life? Is it one of a pair that have become separated somehow? If it is valuable, will it consider itself superior to the plaster cat sitting beside it?

The kitchen, too, is a treasure house of characters waiting to be born. A broken teapot, a kettle which takes a long time to boil, a huge saucepan which is hardly ever used can all have stories locked away beneath their lids.

Step into your garden or local park and the choice widens. An empty birds' nesting box, a frog or lizard in the pond, the childlike stone figure holding aloft the birdbath. How do they react, once given life, to changes in the weather, their habitat and one another?

New characters may be discovered lurking in the most unlikely places. Wherever you go, carry a small notebook. A few scribbled words will serve as a reminder, for it is a well known fact that a neglected idea has a habit of dying, never to be reborn.

Museums and antique shops are crammed with ideas for your character list. You may find an exquisite waxen headed, sad faced doll. What adventures coloured her existence in days gone by? How did she arrive at her present location, and why? In a modern toyshop you may discover a character doll, a train set, contemporary action figure or computer game or a train set. They, too, can spring to life at the touch of your pen.

To find other ideas, try animal watching. Cats, dogs, birds or their larger cousins at the zoo, each will spawn a million ideas ready to be woven into stories for the young reader, many of which along the way will become aids to learning for both you and the child.

Perhaps you enjoy holidays on the beach. If so, look around and listen. Watch the child's concentrated involvement with rock pools, shells, sandcastles and the sea itself. Consider the hundreds of tiny living creatures who make their homes in the sand. Think about the changing moods, the shallows, depths and power of the sea itself. There are a million stories in the ocean waiting to be told. Think yourself into the wonderful world of make believe which surrounds the games children play, and once again story ideas will fill the pages of your notebook.

Things which happen in your daily life can provide good ideas for stories. The birth of a new baby in the family – how do the other children react? An outing or holiday with grandparents – how do the young see their relationships with the older generation, do they have more fun or do they long to return home? Moving house can be traumatic for the adults, what about the children? Do they resent or welcome the change and why?

Characters for this younger age group are limitless. It is perfectly acceptable to create a teddy with a talent for walking the tightrope, or a kite who tugs too hard at its string and flies away to adventure.

As I have mentioned, some comics in this age group continue to accept stories concerning fairies and elves with the traditional background of dragons, castles and magic spells. Nowadays however an editor would be more intrigued were the Fairy King to have received an eviction order from his castle, the fairy to be grounded for dangerous low level flying or the dragon to fail miserably at each new job to which his local Job Centre sends him.

Despite the fact that classic fairy stories are still in demand, bear in mind when considering the wee folk as characters that today's average pre-school child watches television. The thirst for excitement, even in the very young viewer, is based on a knowledge wider than ever before, promoting avid interest in characters ranging from everyday adventures to those featured in space fantasy cartoons, which are currently the order of the day.

ANTHROPOMORPHISATION

Stories for the read-aloud age group are not always centred around animated objects or the wee folk. Stories concerning children similar to the reader in an everyday setting have an equal appeal, particularly if the central character is seen to be doing familiar things in familiar settings. A lonely small child, a little girl with measles, a boy on holiday with relatives, twins and their first day at playschool and many more can all be added to your list of characters.

It is at this point in the readership age range that the author often stops to consider the advisability of replacing a central human character with an anthropomorphised animal facing a parallel dilemma.

Some problems are best dealt with in this way, as it comfortably removes the mind of the reader from the world of harsh fact to that of fictional acceptability. For example, a puppy dog can behave in a naughty fashion, resulting in his becoming lost. The story will obviously end happily in your character's reunion with his family but the character can be seen to display abilities which a child of an equivalent age could not logically possess. The message, however, will still come over loud and clear.

Wind In The Willows contains many excellent examples of this useful technique. The child relates to the seemingly ageless characters who, in animal form, can drive irresponsibly, wage physical war upon the bad guys and generally live out the fantasies which are so necessary to the mind of the developing reader. Characters like Mr Toad can behave like naughty children, despite the fact that they are endowed with all the trappings of the adult world such as their own home and possessions. For the fictional humanised animal, adult responsibilities never dull the edge of those irresponsibly childlike facets of his nature guaranteed to endear him to his young reader.

The technique of anthropomorphisation, or investing with human qualities, has the added benefit of making your story acceptable to a far wider age group. *Watership Down* for example, crosses the age barrier several times and has been read with enjoyment by a great many adults. This hardhitting, and at times horrific, tale deals with the harsher side of life from prejudice and dispossession to the grim reality of death. Were these to be applied to a living, breathing human child, then the whole thing would be too close to home for the comfort of the average young reader.

THOUGHT JOGGERS

Many characters have been drawn from magazine illustrations and advertisements, and particularly from Christmas and birthday cards. Throughout December, as the cards arrive, look at each one to see whether the characters on the front say something to you. Scan each illustration for that seed of inspiration you know instinctively can be nurtured into a picture strip or text story. A humorous Santa Claus, a baby fawn and its mother sheltering beneath the snow laden branches of a fir tree, a robin on a cracked flower pot, children dressing a Christmas tree or a beautiful but deserted garden seen through an open gateway may all fire the imagination and be set aside for future use. Mark each one with a pencil cross on the back to be separated after Christmas from their less interesting companions and stored in a large cardboard box labelled *Thought joggers.*

Someone who once organised a jumble sale once set aside at the end of the afternoon, a pile of unsold annuals dating back to the 1920s. Not only did they make fascinating reading, but it became obvious how the world of the child had changed over the intervening years and they provided a whole new list of characters which had only to be updated and placed in modern day situations to come alive again in children's fiction.

Many of today's stories are traditional tales retold, updating both characters and setting and often including an element of humour that was not found in the original. Folk stories such as *Cinderella* and *Little Red Riding Hood* are given regular facelifts to renew their appeal to the next generation of readers.

Names will often suggest a character. A newly opened children's dress shop seen from the top of a bus had emblazoned across its frontage the name *Swaggerpants* – and in due course *Swaggerpants* became a rather conceited tiger who had a lesson in humility to learn before the story was ended. Having been introduced to a Mr R. Bolt, a writer discovered that he was known to his friends as Rusty; eventually Rusty Bolt became the lazy squire to Sir Clankabout in a nonsense poem.

Additional or secondary characters should be kept to a minimum for the young reader. They should possess clearly defined virtues or vices and be endowed with simple names. It is, incidentally, wise to avoid several names beginning with the same letter; Jenny, Jackie and Josie in one short story will soon lead to confusion. But in other circumstances, the same alliteration will prove acceptable, as in the case of the twins, Peter and Pauline; Pinkie and Perkie and of course, Tweedledum and Tweedledee.

Names should typify the character whenever possible. Barnaby Bear will suggest a solid, good natured creature, Bumble Bear might be clumsy or forgetful, Billy Bear, a schoolboy character and a teutonic bear might become Boris, or B.J. Bear become an American. Alliteration when used in this manner will serve to anchor the character securely in the child's mind.

The rules of the game alter subtly as the reader matures. The central character, the one with whom you have influenced the reader to identify, will need to have more complex strengths and weaknesses. To catch and hold reader interest, your central character will, ideally, be a child of around the same age as the group for which the book is destined and you, as the writer and creator of this individual, must get to know him or her as thoroughly as possible. Your character analysis has a large degree of logic, as you will see from the suggested characterisation notes which, in my opinion, are invaluable:

Name:	Sarah Jennings
Address:	Middletown, a large new town
Age:	12½
Place of Birth:	Bedding-in-the-Wold, a tiny north Essex village
Mother's occupation:	Part-time shop assistant
Father's occupation:	Carpenter with large building firm
Position in family:	Only child
Height:	5ft
Hair:	Red, short, curly
Eyes:	Green
Face:	Pretty, oval, freckles
Accent:	Rural, Essex
Likes:	Horses, country walks and birdlife
Dislikes:	Present location, town and school
Problem:	Enforced removal from country to town by need for father's work. Beginning at new school in second year, when friendships have already been forged. Feels isolated, odd one out. Becomes butt for some girl's spite.

As you can see, as the character builds, her type becomes apparent and you will find yourself improving upon the basic notes you have made as you flesh the character to the point where she will begin to write her own story.

Sarah's vulnerability is something with which every child will sympathise, for it is a common belief among this age group that they are underestimated, underprivileged and generally misunderstood by the adult world.

It is obvious that, eventually, our heroine will achieve happiness. As an only child of busy, hardworking parents, she will need to look to her own inner strength to combat the loneliness and isolation she understandably feels. As, throughout the story, she is seen to overcome the problems which beset her life, the reader will experience a growing empathy with your central character, willing her to succeed and sharing each of her triumphs.

Inevitably, a situation will arise where she will be given the opportunity to bring about the comeuppance of her enemies, to dumbfound her critics, to forge lifelong friendships, and generally to win the day.

Remember that position in the family can play an important part in the moulding of your central character. The youngest child, whilst regarded on the one hand with a tolerant affection by the older children in the family, will also be left out of things, be the recipient of hand downs of anything from clothes to toys or even be bullied into accepting the blame for minor mischievousness in the belief that, being little, he or she stands a better chance of getting away with it than does an older child who should know better.

The middle child of three could experience an even more difficult passage through life for he is neither one thing nor the other, never given the certainty of the older child nor the adult attention of the younger. This factor in itself can be the starting point for many a story.

Not all children are brilliant athletes or academics, but most shine in some area or another. Take the teenager who was influenced, largely due to the interest of his parents in Morris dancing, to become part of a junior group. Although it clearly delighted him to perform locally, he dreaded that his parents and those few trusted friends who were party to his secret, would let it be known that he was a Morris dancer. Eventually, his secret leaked out, and for several weeks he was subjected to ridicule by the less intelligent of his peers. His moment of triumph came when an enlightened schoolteacher asked him to give what proved to be a well informed talk on the history and intricacies of the dance. In that moment, despite a faltering beginning, he won a new respect from the majority of his classmates which effectively silenced any further harassment.

When writing for teenagers, therefore, it is not only neces-sary to be able to create your character but fully to under-stand and identify with the complex emotions which accompany the onset of puberty.

As every parent who has seen their child through adoles-cence knows, these few years must surely be the most difficult they will have to endure. The agonies through which they pass vary only a little between the sexes. They are wracked by self-doubt, unable to comprehend at what point they will cease to be a child and break free from the chrysalis to spread their wings as young men or women.

The average adult could be forgiven for not believing that the adolescent's appearance is of prime importance not only to their own critical eye but also to that of their peers. Personal hygiene, particularly with boys, is of little or no importance until the moment they discover the attraction of the opposite sex. This discovery, however, leads to despair at the first sight of a blackhead or spot, which seemingly occurs at precisely the wrong moment in a budding relationship.

At this age, acne is considered terminal, energy is reserved for discos or sports practice and is totally lacking when there is a need to tidy a bedroom or help with the washing up.

The belief that money grows on trees, and that one's parent need only to reach up to pluck the occasional handful, is evident in their requests for the essential designer trainers and jeans which, you will be assured, every one of their friends possess.

Adolescents seem to lose their ability to communicate with anyone but their own immediate circle of friends. Parental concern over the monosyllabic answers to perfectly natural questions is often greeted with no more than a scowl or a shrug. Many a despairing mother or father, however, has survived these years along with the adolescent to see them emerge, unbelievably, into perfectly normal, healthy adults, enjoying a secure relationship and eventually, producing embryonic adults of their own.

The point has been made that it is the world around the child and not the child itself which has altered over the years. But to be fair, the changes in society which have come about in the last twenty years have had an enormous impact and have produced changes in outlook and attitude, particularly among this age group.

At one time, formal education was completed by the age of fifteen or sixteen, and upon leaving school employment was easy to find. The pattern has changed drastically in recent years. The system now encourages young people to extend their education in the hope that a better qualification will ensure a better start to their working life. Whilst excellent in theory, an increasing number of young people have had to face the fact that, with or without qualifications, they are unable to find a job. A new and very real element of frustration and despair has been added to the adolescent's life and must be reflected in the writer's work if the characters about whom he writes are to have that ring of authenticity.

When creating characters for a teenage story, it therefore becomes essential to know your readers and the world in which they live. There are many organisations which will welcome the help of a responsible adult, such as the Scouting and Girl Guide movement, youth clubs and sports teams. These aim to provide youngsters not only with coaching in their pursuits but also with counselling. Once involved, you will soon discover that every teenager has problems which, to them, appear insurmountable.

If this is the age group that you have chosen to write for, then consider how the character develops as it takes on board new interests and areas of development. Girls often become interested at quite an early age in teenage romance, whilst boys leave emotional involvement on the shelf for a little longer, preferring to direct their energies into the world of sport. Recognise these differences when creating your characters and plot, for this is the stuff of which teenage tales are made.

Stay away from stereotypes. A grandmother can be embarrassingly modern, bad-tempered or unwelcoming (in other words, more interesting) than the apple-cheeked, pie-baking figure so acceptable in bygone years. Parents, too, should be seen to live their own lives, have their own opinions, be deeply involved in their working lives. Far removed, in fact, from the understanding, tolerant, quietly spoken and stereotyped character that once commonly inhabited the pages of a children's book.

Your central characters must never be totally without fault. They will of course have their strengths, but also endow them with a temper, with vanity, or perhaps with a terror of heights or enclosed spaces. All of these will serve to help your reader identify with the characters and so bring your story to life.

One of today's best known writers said he would never consider putting pen to paper until the characters he had created could be heard, quite literally, to take their first breath, until he felt that double heartbeat within himself that guaranteed his characters would come to life with equal conviction in the mind of the reader.

Once you experience this uncanny moment, you will come to realise that the groundwork undertaken in the creation of your character, on both a physical and emotional level, is well worthwhile. You must know every facet of your character, regard him or her as an iceberg, the top of which may be reported and therefore apparent to your reader, but the bulk of which lies below the waterline. This is of major importance and, like the iceberg, is the stabilising factor without which your character cannot convincingly exist.

As a readership survey across the various age groups brought to light, a definite preference is for books written from the main character's point of view but in the third person, and this technique is preferred by authors and editors alike.

The character in the following excerpt from my own book

Final Curtain is well established in the first three hundred words, using the third person viewpoint:

It was late afternoon as Robin Botham boarded the train. Christmas holidays past and school due to begin again the following day, he faced the inevitable with mixed feelings. The thought of returning to face the taunting Bull Harmsworth churned familiarly at his stomach as he made his formal farewells to his father.

'Now, stiff upper lip lad. Don't let 'em get you down. Home again before long, eh?'

The boy looked down from the carriage window into the face of a stranger. Was it only two years since his mother's death? Robin frowned away the lump that still, at times like this, threatened to choke him, remembering the laughing blue eyes, summer walks and secret games that belonged to happier times.

His father, always a background figure he now realised, had withdrawn further from the child, silenced by his own grief until, as if anxious to turn his back from all that could remind him, he sent Robin away to school.

'It's the best there is, lad,' he had said, staring into the fire, 'Went there myself. Bit hard at first but you'll soon get the hang of it.'

But Robin didn't. The qualities inherited from his gentle mother, the soft voice, shy manner and love of beauty were no safeguard from the thugs of the world and true to type, the worst of their kind at the school, Bull Harmsworth, homed in on the defenceless new arrival. Three terms had now passed and each worse than before. Apart from the menial tasks he was forced to perform for his tormentor, he found himself the butt for the older boy's spiteful humour.

'Bottom,' he would yell down the corridors, 'Get your backside in here.' He delighted his cronies with jokes on a similar theme. 'You're a bum,' he would crow, fuelled by Robin's misery until, released at last, the child would sob silently into his pillow, yearning for the lost warmth of his mother's arms.

The lurch of the moving train brought a look of relief to his father's and Robin's face alike. There was really nothing to say except 'Goodbye'.

FIRST OR THIRD PERSON VIEWPOINT

As you can see, the reader is made aware of the child's appearance, his emotional vulnerability, past history and the further miseries which await him on his return to school. Similarly, Bull Harmsworth's character is shown to the reader with just a few lines of telling dialogue.

Whilst most stories for children are written in the third person, first person viewpoint has its uses and is regularly employed to sharpen the reader's appreciation of the involvement of the central character, most noticeably in teenage romance and tales of the supernatural for older children.

When writing in the first person, the writer relies heavily on interaction between the characters to convey the personality of the central *I* figure. His or her reaction to other characters in the story will provide the means by which the writer can convey likes, dislikes, physical attributes, hopes and desires.

The following encounter from the title story of *Final Curtain*, provides an illustration of this point when the central character, a starstruck teenage girl working on the production of a play, overhears a conversation between the male lead and his understudy.

'So, when I say jump, you jump. All right, boyo?'

I'd have known that Welsh baritone anywhere. Grant Davis was taking someone apart at the seams by the sound of it.

'And another thing. Just because you're my understudy, don't think this is a shortcut to stardom. You'll stay where you belong – in the wings. Just you remember, you young puppy, I'm the star of this production.'

There was a click and the door nearest to me swung inward, revealing a red-faced young man.

He mumbled something and stepped dejectedly from the trailer, almost onto my foot. I opened my mouth to apologise. After all, I had been eavesdropping but the words died in my throat.

I found myself looking into the bluest eyes I have ever seen. I noticed at that same moment, the strong chin, laughing mouth, square shoulders and dark curly hair and for a minute, I felt quite weak at the knees.

He grinned ruefully, 'I suppose you heard all that.'

I nodded dumbly, noticing for the first time the dimple at the side of his curved lips.

'He's not easy to work with,' he whispered, 'I just hope the female lead is a bit more friendly.'

I found my voice suddenly, although it sounded a couple of octaves higher for some reason, 'Jane Foulton? Oh, she's as nice as she is beautiful.'

What a daft thing to say! I could have kicked myself.

His eyes lit up with interest, 'Do you know her then?'

'N-no,' now I looked a complete idiot, 'It's just what I heard.'

'Oh, that publicity rubbish they had out. Yes, I've heard it too. She's probably stuck-up and big-headed. After all, to be a big name at nineteen has got to have gone to her head.'

'That's not fair!' I exclaimed, 'I've seen her act and she's got more talent in her little finger than... you've probably got in your whole body.'

Now I'd really blown it, I told myself, as I saw his brow darken angrily.

'Since you're obviously such a fan of hers, I apologise,' he said stiffly, 'To both of you!' and turning on his heel, he strode away.

I watched him go, feeling I'd just let the whole world slip through my clumsy fingers.

Within a story like this, which is aimed at young teenage girls, the reader can clearly identify with the feelings of the central *I* character. Old enough to be more than a little attracted to the young man, her behaviour betrays her immaturity. She is clearly at that awkward stage between girl and womanhood, longing to be sophisticated enough to impress the opposite sex but well aware that she has a good way to go before this happy condition can be achieved.

Once you have decided upon your character, do a detailed analysis as outlined earlier, transferring a thumbnail sketch to the first column of your story planner. By now, you know what constitutes the type in the second column and will, in all probability, have a fairly clear outline of the problem with which your character must come to terms.

More than one character is almost certain to form in your mind and soon the columns of your notebook will have become satisfyingly full, so that a glance through it will cause your mind to be teeming with ideas for the next step which is constructing a plot fit for your character.

6
PROBLEMS AND SOLUTIONS

Difficulty gives all things their estimation.
Montagne

Characters make plots and having established your character and its type, it is time for the next move, which is to pinpoint your character's major problem.

Your notebooks have served their purpose as a collecting house and it is time for them to be put to one side for future reference. The characters you have chosen to work with can now be transferred to your plotting file. For this purpose, an A4 ringbinder is ideal, into which can be inserted loose-leaf pages ruled into columns in which the necessary component parts of your story will be listed.

Head the columns: Character (Name); Nature; Problem; Solution. Perhaps your first character will be a doll called Belinda: in the next column, establish that she is old and tattered. First give her a nice nature and then, to provide a second story for the character, endow her with a spiteful, envious streak. Under Problem bring into play your second character, a beautiful modern character doll called Samantha, with flowing locks, an improbable figure and a wardrobe of clothes that would rival a Hollywood soap, who arrives and takes up residence in the toy cupboard alongside Belinda. The solution to each of the two stories will be different due to Belinda's nature.

Let us assume that the older doll probably belonged to the mother of the little girl who now owns her. For as long as the other toys can remember, Belinda has been the one they have turned to for kindness, understanding and wisdom. If she has

77

a nice nature, it is unlikely that her faded silk dress and battered straw hat would be of any importance to her. Until, that is, Samantha arrives in the toy cupboard. The new doll is feted and adored by the other toys, while Belinda is forced to realise that, alongside her new rival, she is shabby and old. Secretly, she wishes that she could command the same degree of admiration. A series of incidents, however, prove that, although the new doll may be beautiful on the outside, alongside Belinda she is vain and dumb. When, one by one, the toys all shun her, she turns to Belinda for comfort, expressing the wish that she were more like the older doll, kinder, wiser and loved by the other toys. Belinda puts things right, teaches the new doll all she needs to know to be accepted and forgiven and makes a friend.

The story would have a far different ending, however, if Belinda had a spiteful, envious disposition. Upon the arrival of the new doll, she sets out to make her as unpopular as possible. Alternatively, and perhaps with the application of a little magic, it would be possible to transform tattered Belinda into a beautiful doll herself. How would it affect her nature and her relationships with the other toys?

Kenny the Kite, another character established for younger readers, allows a great deal more freedom for, although he may live part of his life rolled up in the corner of the toy cupboard, he really comes alive on a windy day, when he can fly free, tugging at his string, diving and weaving in the bright blue sky.

Under Nature could be listed *naughty*, *nervous*, *adventurous* and *brave*. A naughty kite could snap its string deliberately and come to grief as a result in a hundred different ways, learning a lesson in obedience. A nervous kite could, perhaps, be afraid of heights and refuse to fly. Here, to complete the solution, Kenny could become tangled in the branches of a tree, where his young owner is forced to leave him overnight. In the early evening, he is discovered by a family of birds learning to fly. The parent birds free him and include Kenny in their flying lessons. He soon realises that there is nothing to be afraid of and waits excitedly for his young owner to retrieve him, so that he can show him how beautifully acrobatic he has become.

An adventurous kite could be torn aloft by accident and could set off to see the world. This, in itself, could possibly give rise to a series of stories, each one both exciting and educational.

A brave kite might be a rather drab affair, made lovingly by his young owner's grandfather from plain paper. When he arrives at the park, he realises that all the other kites are brightly coloured and while he is flying aloft, the others begin to tease him because he is so plain. He flies towards some trees to get away from them and hears the plaintive cry of a kitten, who is trapped high up in one of the branches. With a great deal of tugging, he manages to hover close to the branch, where the terrified kitten is clinging. Then brave Kenny has an idea. He loops the loop, tying his string firmly around the branch. By now, his young owner is at the foot of the tree and sees what has happened. The park keeper is called and rescues both kitten and Kenny but sadly, Kenny is torn. Grandfather takes him home and repairs him but this time, he paints him in bright colours with a big smiling face in the middle of the kite. Next time he is flown in the park, all the other kites say how handsome he is and how clever he was to rescue the kitten.

DEVELOPING THE CHARACTER

Now let us return to Belinda. As the oldest inhabitant of the toy cupboard, she has ruled the roost unopposed, using her superior knowledge and wisdom to dominate the other toys apparently in a benevolent manner. The new doll, Samantha, is a breath of fresh air to the other toys but clearly a rival to Belinda who, to the toys' dismay, exhibits a side of her nature which has not before been apparent. Once challenged, she becomes jealous and spiteful, causing the other toys to desert her in favour of Samantha.

At this point, the child's affection for Belinda will begin to wane and they will find themselves on the side of the bright new intruder, when once they felt an initial animosity.

The child's sense of justice, however, will not allow the

writer to dispose of Belinda by, for example, giving her away to a jumble sale. This would produce a most unsatisfactory conclusion, for they will draw a parallel with their own behaviour – the writer would be saying to them, 'if you are naughty, you will be sent away.'

It would be necessary, therefore, for Samantha to find some way of healing the breach with Belinda and the rest of the toys, perhaps by deliberately creating a situation to which only Belinda is able to offer a solution. In these circumstances, Belinda's ego would be repaired, the toys forced to admit that they cannot do without her and the older doll brought to the realisation that being nasty does not pay.

This solution would be satisfying to the young reader as it will subconsciously draw a parallel, yet again, with its own behaviour, where an admission of guilt and an apology, in almost every case, evokes forgiveness.

Stories of this type for the younger reader can often be the spoonful of sugar that helps the medicine (contained in a moral) go down. Naughty Kenny the Kite is an example of the dangers a child might encounter if it runs away from Mum whilst shopping. The nervous Kenny the Kite teaches the lesson that nothing is impossible, given a little courage and a lot of guidance. The plain paper Kenny points out quite clearly that beauty is only skin deep and it is the quality of bravery that is of prime importance.

PLANNING

When dealing with real animals, your characters should be subjected to problems similar to those encountered by their wild counterparts. They should also exhibit the same tendencies. Foxes are invariably portrayed as being sly; deer, nervous; lions, fearless; moles, short-sighted and owls, wise. Each aspect of their nature will, in itself, provide sufficient problem material for your storyline.

Stories centred around children in everyday settings, involved in everyday activities are, you may feel, more difficult to write. Certainly, they require thought. You cannot, for example, solve their problems by the use of magic, neither

Plotting Chart

1 Character	2 Nature	3 Problem	4 Solution
Tattered old doll (Belinda)	Nice nature	Beautiful new doll Samantha arrives in toy cupboard	Belinda realises beauty is only skin deep and helps new doll to settle in.
	Spiteful, envious	Samantha and Belinda become enemies	Belinda is forced to learn a lesson and the dolls become friends.
Kenny the Kite	Naughty	Snaps string deliberately	Is rescued in nick of time – moral: don't run away.
	Nervous	Refuses to fly	Helped to overcome fear by family of birds.
	Adventurous	Off to see the world (possible series)	'Littlest Hobo' character landing in various locations to help solve children's problems.
	Brave but plain appearance	Rescues kitten from tree but gets caught in branches and is torn	Is mended and learns it's not in how he looks but how he behaves that is important.

can you resolve an impossible situation by saying, 'And then little Tommy woke up. It had all been a terrible dream.' They are, however, increasingly popular with children's publishers, many of whom categorically state that they are unprepared to consider cuddly clouds, buzzy bees or friendly flowers. By using your imagination, you can create a problem situation which can be rectified by natural, and therefore acceptable, means and you will have a saleable story and as with every other field of writing, no matter who or what your central character, if it is skilfully crafted it will eventually sell.

Work through your list of characters, problems and solutions in this manner. Do not stop to agonise if an idea does not come to mind immediately, simply jot down your first thoughts. Once you have acquired the necessary techniques, ideas will flow more readily. Take care when completing the final column in your file, for whatever your adult mind might see as the solution, it must be logical and acceptable to the young reader.

If, however, you force-feed your reader with the moral tale, you will lose him. Remember, children hate to be talked down to, so be quite sure you are not wagging a warning finger at them when you write.

SEVERAL CHARACTERS – HOW MANY PROBLEMS?

By now, it should be clear that, for younger children, simplicity is the key word. One central character, together with a minimum supporting cast and an uncomplicated background to your story will provide an enjoyable and untaxing story for your reader. As we take the next step into the world inhabited by the nine year old child and into a teenage readership, the ground rules alter noticeably. Gone are the anthropomorphised dolls and kites and, in their place, the writer begins to deal with realism.

Richmal Crompton's *Just William* stories, although dated by today's standards, nonetheless incorporate a family structure and characterisation still used by contemporary writers.

William is a typical boy of the period, scruffy, undisciplined, eternally hungry and the leader of a gang of equally disreputable boys of his own age. The attitude of William's teenage sister is one of haughty intolerance, the father's attitude is one of exasperation, while his mother's acceptance of his behaviour seems to be largely due to her preoccupation with other matters. Ginger is William's willing partner in crime, while Violet Elizabeth Bott dotes adoringly on the scruffy little rascal.

At this stage in its reader growth the child is not only able to cope with the addition of one or more sub-plots, but actually demands the involvement of all other characters who have a bearing upon the central character in the story.

The sub-plot or back story for many of William's exploits is provided by the adult characters in the book who, through their apparent inability to remember what it was like to be young, force William into situations from which he emerges unscathed, more by luck than judgement.

Richmal Crompton exhibited great skill as a children's writer by keeping William in the forefront of each of his adventures. He was always the catalyst and always the victor, creating that essential balance without which the secondary characters, no matter how lively and contributory to the storyline, would nevertheless be unable to exist.

This type of story is one which can easily bridge the generations to be brought to life in a similar set of adventures for today's young reader.

There is a shift yet again, however, in the basic rules of writing for children when considering the teenage market brought about largely by the change in the attitudes of the teenager of today. Whilst the same techniques are employed with regard to characterisation, plotting becomes a far more subtle process. Where it would never occur to a character of William's type to try and analyse his parents' thoughts or feelings, a teenage character would be heavily emotionally involved in any problems his or her family may be experiencing.

To illustrate the point, let us return to the previous chapter and our character analysis of Sarah Jennings. At 12½ years of age, Sarah is in the middle of her vulnerable years. Uprooted from the familiarity of her beloved country background, she finds herself in a large new town, forced to break new ground and to forge new friendships in a new school.

These problems in themselves would be enough to occupy the mind of the central character but the back story will contain many other factors which will prove to have a direct bearing on her young life. Her parents, too, find themselves in a new situation. Her mother's job as a part-time shop assistant will not be without influence, if only because it means she is absent from home on Sarah's daily return from school. The mother may well become ill, placing a burden on the shoulders of the young central character. Her father may be made redundant, bringing into play a shortage of money, the possibility of house repossession, the embarrassment of having a father on Social Security and the change of mood within the home.

Sarah will feel all of these additional pressures whilst the main storyline will be one of the girl's ability to make a place for herself within the new and initially unfriendly location. The back story will provide many of the obstacles which must be overcome along the way. As an only child, Sarah must use her own strength to find a way to achieve both stability and happiness, for she cannot, out of a sense of loyalty, add her own problems to those of her parents.

The eventual solution may well, inadvertently, lead to a happy conclusion on all fronts in just the same way as in a story for younger readers, but the exploration of the fast-maturing emotions of your teenage reader will have been essential to the storyline.

TIMESCALE

It may well be that, due to the timespan covered by your story, your central character will mature within that scale. Attitudes and beliefs in the teenager undergo a major change in the space of a twelvemonth and so will those of your character. In order to maintain pace, and therefore reader interest, the action of your story should ideally take place over a minimal period. A few weeks, or at the most months, should be sufficient to establish the characterisation, problem and solution pattern of the story. Few books written for this age group cover a period of several years in the life of the central character but should the author find it necessary to use a timespan of these proportions, then attention should be paid to the gradual but all-important process of maturity both on a physical and emotional level.

In similar vein, if you are considering a historical or timeslip background to your tale, bear in mind the importance of accuracy of detail. Apart from costume and location, a thorough investigation should be made into the social pressures imposed upon children during the relevant period.

No matter how strong your character or excellent your story, it is unlikely it will find its way into print unless you can entice your publisher into reading beyond the first page. It is essential therefore to set your main character firmly into time and place on the first page, and to grab your reader's attention in no uncertain terms – preferably in the first paragraph.

Love her or loathe her, it is nevertheless still possible to learn from the well worn pen of Enid Blyton how to get straight into a story. Take the first line of her book *Amelia Jane Again!*:

> Now once the toys in the nursery had a party and they didn't ask that big naughty doll, Amelia Jane.

The expert Enid, in a mere twenty words, portrays the setting, the mood, the name and the personality of her central character in a way that has you eager and willing to find out more about Amelia Jane. Who is she, why do the other toys consider her to be naughty and what has she done to cause her to be left out of a party? Already the child reader will experience a degree of sympathy with the big doll.

Award winning author Dick King-Smith employs a similar technique in the first line of his book *The Water Horse*:

> It was Kirstie who found it. It was lying just above the high water mark...

Once again, you know where and who but you just have to

read on if you want to know what and why.

David Wiseman's recent publication for younger readers *Mum's Winning Streak* begins with the intriguing words: It all started on holiday when Angie found a four-leafed clover.

Who could resist reading on to find out what started and in what holiday location? The four-leaf clover in itself suggests an element of magic in the tale waiting to be told.

Climbing steadily up the age range, the need for an intriguing opening line grows even stronger. Historical novelist Rosemary Sutcliff demonstrates her skill in *The Shield Ring* with the opening words: The thing happened with the appalling swiftness of a hawk swooping out of a quiet sky...

Simply by reading these few first words you immediately have a sense of the period in which the book is set, as well as the mood of the first chapter, which is clearly menacing and promises thrilling adventure.

A final example is produced by one of the nation's finest authors, Charles Dickens. His opening to *A Christmas Carol* provides a superb illustration of the use of simple, clear language powerfully to grab and hold the reader's attention:

> Marley was dead: to begin with. There is no doubt whatever about that. The register of his burial was signed by the clergyman, the clerk, the undertaker, and the chief mourner. Scrooge signed it; and Scrooge's name was good upon 'Change, for anything he chose to put his hand to. Old Marley was as dead as a door-nail.

There cannot be a person living of reading age who does not know the story of Scrooge, appearing as it does on our television screens during each Christmas period. No matter how lavish the production, most lovers of Dickens would agree that the filmmakers have yet to capture the impact of Dickens' written word to complete satisfaction. A point well-illustrated in the foregoing paragraph. In a few words, once again, the scene is set, the character established and the reader made aware that here is a tale worth telling.

THE SOLUTION – TYING LOOSE ENDS

However, no matter how the attention of the reader is caught and held, nothing provides more satisfaction than a solution which ties together all the loose ends, crosses all the t's and dots every i. As an example, think again about the Kenny the Kite story where his nature is brave.

In this simple plot, we first have the grandfather painstakingly making a plain kite for his grandson to fly in the park. When the kite is damaged, the first loose end is tied into place by Kenny's repair and subsequent redecoration. The second problem is that Kenny, due to his colourless design, becomes the butt of the other kites' teasing. This aspect is solved by, on one hand, their subsequent admiration for Kenny's bravery and, on the other, by his splendid new appearance.

The third problem is the deflation of Kenny's initial pride, resulting in his running for the trees to hide. The solution is that, his cowardice forgotten, he exhibits bravery to save the kitten, thereby risking personal damage and possibly total destruction. The glaring loose end which would be ignored at the author's peril is that the kitten must be returned safely to its owner, thereby bringing about a happy ending for all concerned.

The middle age range reader, having been involved by the author in a more complex plot, will be aware of even more loose ends when they are skilfully woven into the closing chapters.

In the *Just William* stories, it was necessary for the author, once having used her central character, albeit inadvertently to cause chaos within his family, to bring about an ending which satisfied the needs of each individual character.

Once the author enters the corridors of realism leading to the teenage mind, things do not fall so happily into place. Transgressions on the part of your central character may be of proportions that are not easily overcome or forgiven and at the end of your story, they may yet have to work towards a solution but a glimmer of hope may be all that is needed to tie a loose end into place.

7
THE FINISHED MANUSCRIPT

Pleasing ware is half sold.

George Herbert

Although we have explored the various age groups and differences which exist between them, these are general guidelines for submitting your completed manuscript that apply to all publishers alike.

It pays to remember, at this point, that arrows are more effective than buckshot and this is where market research (dealt with in Chapter Three) pays off.

Whilst you will, over the years, compile and regularly update your own list of possible markets, you will find a list of helpful addresses in Chapter Twelve.

Many novice writers make the mistake of offering their work for approval to members of the family and close friends. Seldom will their criticism, unless they themselves are published writers, have any value. Their desire to please or encourage you, or indeed to displease or discourage you, will be based upon the relationship which currently exists and their lack of knowledge about the techniques involved.

Manuscript appraisal prior to offering the finished work to a publisher can be obtained by some agents but it is wise to query, before posting off your precious offering, whether or not they charge a reader's fee. Obtaining professional criticism in this way may prove to be expensive, particularly if you send your work to a professional reading agency. Any novice writer contemplating approaching such an agency would be well advised to check their credentials thoroughly and to be sure about charges and the service on offer before parting with any manuscripts.

A far better way to obtain worthwhile criticism is to join a creative writing class sponsored by your local adult education authority. Contact your local library who will give you details of any classes of this nature in your area. Here, you will receive not only tuition in the techniques of writing but a fair and unbiased criticism by your tutor of work you produce during the term.

As you involve yourself more deeply in both reading the published work of other authors, and in producing your own manuscripts, you will with time become your own best critic.

An excellent way of judging your own work is to read the first draft onto a tape recorder then, with your manuscript in front of you and your highlighter pen poised, listen to the recorded tape. Repetition and omissions will become immediately apparent and, once highlighted, will show the areas of weakness and need for repair.

Remember that editorial guidelines will also contain details of the required content and will be very relevant to the age and target group of the potential readership.

Another important factor will, however, be the lead times, particularly in the case of newspapers, magazines and comics. Articles and short stories with a seasonal flavour need to be on the editor's desk some months in advance of the publication date. As a rough guide, for these individual markets, allow two weeks for daily newspapers, four weeks for weekly newspapers and at least six weeks for weekly colour supplements. For magazines, allow six weeks for weeklies, three months for monthlies and six months for quarterlies.

Stories with a seasonal flavour are always in demand in the magazine and newspaper markets. Annual slots on the calendar such as Easter, Halloween and Christmas must be filled and hard-pressed editors are often on the lookout for original seasonal storylines. By ensuring that such manuscripts arrive on the editorial desk well in advance of the publication date, you will increase your chances of a sale. Stories for Christmas, for example, should be in the editor's hands by the end of July at the latest, so it is a good idea to keep a year diary, marking off high days and holidays and their related manuscript submission dates.

Should it be your intention to write a full-length book, forward planning on the part of the author can often increase the chance of acceptance. Books are produced in time for specific publication dates, taking from six months to a year to produce plus at least three months from your first letter of enquiry to acceptance and contract. If you intend to cover an anniversary such as, for example, Shakespeare's birth or an event similar to the one which featured prominently throughout 1992, the anniversary of Columbus's discovery of America, your manuscript should be completed and submitted for publication approximately eighteen months in advance of the anniversary date.

PRESENTATION

The first rule when submitting a manuscript is that, if you wish your work to be read by an editor, make it worth reading. Put yourself for a moment in the shoes of an editor faced on a Monday morning with a mountain of unsolicited manuscripts, some neatly typed and clipped to a polite covering letter and others handwritten on dog-eared pages. Which would you choose to read first? Which, regardless of its content, would give you the most pleasure to handle? Handwritten submissions rarely, if ever, meet with success and it is understandable that a busy editor, faced with a pile of manuscripts will select for his consideration one which is pleasing and easy to read, rather than a scrawled and scruffy offering.

Your manuscript should be typed in double line spacing on standard A4 typing paper between margins 2" wide on the left and 1" wide on the right. It will pass through many hands once accepted and these margins are used to accommodate the editor's comments, typesetting instructions or notes to the illustrator. Use only one side of the paper and always take a carbon copy or, if using a word-processor, keep a back up disk or run off an extra draft to keep on file.

The first page should have at its top right hand corner your name, address and telephone number. In the centre of the page, approximately one third of the way down, immediately above the first lines of the text, should be the title underlined in block capitals and below that should appear a note of the approximate length of the manuscript. This length can easily be calculated by counting the words in five random lines on one page and dividing the total by five, arriving at the average number of words in a line. This number, multiplied by the number of full-length lines in your manuscript, will give an approximate word count. If you have a word-processor, the number of k per file used will give you a rough indication of the approximate number of words. Using a Locoscript 2 program on an Amstrad word-processor, for example, 4k would, at a rough estimate equal approximately 300 words: 10k, 1,000 words; 18k, 2,000 words: 24k , 3,000 words: 32k, 4,000 words and 40k, 5,000 words. Always round the figure up or down to the nearest whole number to give it the professional touch. To state an exact figure is the mark of an amateur.

Each successive page must bear the title, author's name and page number clearly across the top. In a book manuscript, the page number from the first page should be numbered consecutively from Page 1 right through the entire manuscript to the final page.

In the bottom right hand corner of each page of all manuscripts, many editors are pleased to see some indication of the fact that further pages exist within the manuscript. A simple *m/f* denoting that *more follows* or the page number followed by the number of pages still to come, for example *6/20*. Picture-strip layout, however, differs slightly and guidelines for this can be found in a later chapter.

Protect your precious manuscript from grime and wear and tear by means of a front and back sheet, the latter being simply a blank piece of paper. A front sheet should bear, in the top right hand corner, your legal name, in other words, the one to whom the cheque should be made payable. Beneath it, your own address and on the left, your telephone number if you have one. In the centre, the title of the manuscript, *Blanche the Rabbit*, for example, followed by an explanation, *A short read-aloud story for 3–5 year olds*, the approximate length *350 words* and your pen name should you wish to use one.

A pen name, otherwise known as a byline, pseudonym or nom de plume is a matter of personal choice. You do not need one to be a writer. If, however, your own name is long and perhaps hard to pronounce, you may wish to choose something short and simple. If you are a woman writing for the boys adventure market, you might feel that a masculine pen name would be more acceptable to the reader. Many well-known writers use several pen names, all of which have been carefully chosen for once having established success, it will become a name they must live with for the remainder of their writing life.

Fastening and packaging your manuscript can be a problem. Generally speaking, editors prefer that a short story or article is secured with a paperclip rather than a staple, as should each individual chapter of a book. There are exceptions to this rule which will become apparent should you establish a lengthy relationship with an editor or publishing house.

The rule of thumb should be commonsense. Some editors prefer the paperclip as a fastener in defence of broken nails which could occur if you had stapled your manuscript together. Others are willing to sacrifice this consideration in order to ensure that pages of your manuscript do not become detached.

To the front of your manuscript should be clipped a brief covering letter to the editor. If it is possible to discover his name, then by all means address him personally. Do not be tempted to tell him your life story, it need say no more than the following:

Dear Editor (name),

I enclose herewith for your consideration a short story entitled 'Blanche the Rabbit' of approximately 350 words, written for the pre-school age group, for which First British Serial Rights are available.

I enclose return postage and look forward to your early reply.

Yours sincerely

Opinions differ concerning the necessity of such a letter but to my mind, it should be included, not only as a matter of courtesy but also to specify the rights you propose to sell, an important aspect which is dealt with later in this chapter.

Return postage must also be included in the form of a stamped self-addressed envelope or, more economically, a large white stamped self-addressed label which can be pasted onto your own envelope in the case of rejection or affixed to a smaller envelope containing an acceptance. Ensure, if the postal charge is above the basic rate, that identical return postage is included as excess postal charges can be more expensive. Remember that without return postage, your manuscript could be lost forever.

When sending book manuscripts, to set your mind at rest that your precious work has reached its intended destination, include a stamped, self-addressed postcard bearing a brief statement of receipt along the lines of: *I acknowledge receipt of your manuscript entitled...*

Where publishers may be slow to send their own acknowledgements they will invariably return these reply paid postcards very quickly.

It is better never to fold your manuscript and, in order to keep its pristine appearance, it is advisable to place it into a folder. The type which finds favour with the busy editor is of the envelope variety in plain card, brightly coloured and clearly marked on the flap with a white label bearing the title of your manuscript.

Plastic folders, whilst slimmer and less expensive, can prove to be a source of irritation; a dozen or more piled one upon the other will, with predictable ease and the slightest movement, slide from the desk to the floor, often spilling their contents in a troublesome heap.

Check list

Before placing your manuscript in its envelope, use the following check list:

1. Having researched the market, are you aiming your manuscript at the right publisher?
2. Is it written to the required length?
3. Have you marked each page clearly with your name, the title of the work and the page number?
4. Does the first page bear your address?
5. Has the front sheet sufficient details clearly to tell the editor what is contained within?
6. Have you included a brief covering letter?
7. Have you attached a self-addressed stamped label?
8. Is the manuscript neatly contained within a folder?
9. Have you checked that the editorial address is currently correct?
10. Have you allowed sufficient postage upon both the outgoing envelope and the return label?

Once your work is signed and sealed, the delivery must be given careful thought as our postal system has been known to make the occasional minor error. A single short story, providing you have retained the all important copy, if lost will not be too difficult to reproduce and re-submit. Never send carbon copies to an editor and, unless you have invested in a word-processor, it is often a good idea to obtain a high quality photocopy of your original to hold in reserve against loss or damage. The manuscript of a full-length book could, however, represent a great deal of unnecessary time and effort to reproduce. Recorded delivery is, I have found, a tried and tested safeguard, one which is well worth using for the modest additional cost involved.

MULTIPLE SUBMISSIONS AND RECORD KEEPING

Where book manuscripts are concerned, it is worth considering multiple submissions – in other words, sending your manuscript to half a dozen publishers at the same time. Ensure that each copy is clear and well presented. Your individual covering letter should explain that the manuscript has also been sent to a number of other publishing houses.

There are some publishers who may object to receiving a manuscript which has been submitted simultaneously to other markets. On the plus side, however, the majority will realise that if the manuscript is of outstanding quality, then they will wish not only to read it without delay but, should it prove acceptable for their list, to make the first offer of purchase to the author.

The process of submission of a manuscript to a publishing house and its subsequent acceptance or rejection can often take three to six months to complete. In order to keep track of your manuscripts, devise a straightforward method of recording their progress. An exercise book, ruled in columns, will suffice, containing a detailed record of when and to whom the manuscript was submitted and the result (which will be the date it was either rejected or accepted). Headings for each column could be: Date sent; Title; Publisher; Accepted; Rejected; Date. In this way, you can see at a glance where your manuscript is at any given time. Some authors prefer a simple card index system which is designed to contain the same information for easy reference.

Once your manuscript has been posted, it is best to busy yourself with the next, for time will hang heavy if you merely sit back and wait for the result. The time will come, however, after a sensible period, when it is perfectly acceptable for you to make a polite enquiry as to its fate.

Generally speaking, a magazine will take between six to eight weeks to come to a decision, although some take considerably longer. If the news for which you are so eagerly waiting concerns a book, then it is unlikely that you will hear anything (other than an acknowledgement of receipt of your manuscript) for at least two to three months. If, however, you have reached the limit of your patience, you may write or telephone the editor.

Should you decide to phone him, you may well get no further than his secretary, the most common stock phrase being 'I'm afraid he's in a meeting. May I take a message?' If you do manage to break through the secretarial barrier, however, the chance to talk to the editor about his requirements and the opportunity to forge a good relationship with him by making it quite clear that you are a professional writer able to take criticism and, if necessary, to rewrite your manuscript to suit his requirements, is of considerable importance.

It is more than possible that, during a discussion of this nature in which you have established a rapport, you will receive some sort of commission. In other words, your initial manuscript has, in fact, met with his approval, you have convinced him that you can deliver reliable material on a regular basis and have persuaded him actually to ask that you produce another manuscript on specific lines.

Should this be the happy outcome, then write to him immediately, confirming the commission and the agreed terms. Once having written and despatched the required manuscript to the editor, you are almost certain of a sale. However, once you have received a letter of acceptance, the editor could be replaced by someone new whose editorial preference differs from that of your initial contact. Should this occur, you may find your manuscript is returned to you unpublished before you have received the promised payment. Your original letter of confirmation to the editor and his subsequent written acceptance of your manuscript can now be used to negotiate what is known as a 'kill fee'. This is an amount payable to an author for work which has been accepted but subsequently never published and usually amounts to half of the initial fee offered. Most reputable publishing houses will, in fact, offer a kill fee together with an apology when they return your unpublished manuscript, but if they do not you will have to take the matter up with the new editor yourself. Once an author has received a kill fee, he is perfectly free to offer that work for sale elsewhere.

COPING WITH REJECTION

If, despite all your efforts, good market research, careful

presentation, well estimated lead times and a well crafted plot, your manuscript is returned, do not despair, you are in good company. Most of the great writers of today have suffered rejection at some stage in their career but they did not let it beat them and neither must you.

A common reason for rejection is that the editor to which you sent your manuscript has recently bought something of a similar nature. Take another look at your manuscript and see whether it can be altered or improved. Some editors will take the trouble to tell you just where you went wrong, so take their advice and put it right.

Whatever the reason, do not automatically assume that because one publishing house has rejected it, your manuscript must be unsaleable. Read it through, alter it if necessary, even retype it but send it to another editor immediately, it may be just what he is looking for.

COPYRIGHT

The arrival of that wonderful letter of acceptance may, however, bring with it hitherto unforeseen problems. Earlier in this chapter, I briefly mentioned the question of publication rights. In Great Britain, copyright protection becomes automatic from the instant that the work is created. There is no necessity to register the manuscript or to pay fees to any organisation.

To establish the author's legal ownership in printed work, the publisher will ensure that on the copyright page of the volume appears the copyright symbol ©, the author's name and the first year of publication. Copyright protects the form in which the idea or storyline is expressed. It does not protect an idea in itself, a plot or theme, or a fact. The author, once having completed the work and thereby having established ownership of the copyright, has then the exclusive right to negotiate its reproduction and publication or, in the case of drama, the permission for the work to be performed in public or to be broadcast or filmed.

A manuscript suitable for adaptation or translation will also require the cooperation and permission of the author as will the granting of a licence in the case of other subsidiary rights, such as those which could be linked to a specific character in the form of toys and games, animation and similar areas of merchandising.

The message then, is clear. Never sell your copyright but only the specific rights as and when they apply. There are one or two notable contradictions to this rule, however, specifically in the area of picture-strip writing, which will be dealt with in Chapter Eight.

Traditionally, an author will offer to the editor of a newspaper, magazine or junior publication, First British Serial Rights or the right to publish once for the first time in this country. In recent years, however, some publishing houses have shown a marked dislike for this practice and have, in turn, either returned the manuscript with a covering letter stating that they do not accept manuscripts on this basis, or they have submitted an offer which clearly states their intentions as to the purchase of rights.

This offer may range from their non-negotiable intention to purchase, for a stated fee, anything, from the right to publish in specific foreign markets as well as those in the UK to 'All Rights For All Purposes' which virtually blankets the author's options established under copyright.

It is the choice of the author to either accept or decline their offer but, before making the final decision, thought should be given to the opportunity it presents.

It may be that the payment is small and that the publisher demands the purchase of all rights which, at first, appears to be a raw deal. If the character is original and has been carefully crafted by the author to have animation and merchandising potential, then he would be a fool to part with those rights to a publisher who would then be free to exploit them for his own gain. Horror tales of now firmly established characters having been sold for a pittance by their originators are legendary.

Learn from their mistakes, but temper your enthusiasm with caution – such an offer may prove to be an opportunity for the novice author to place his foot upon the first rung of a ladder and to establish a regular market for similar work over a period of time. The discipline involved, the experience gained and resultant portfolio of published work can, in itself, outweigh the disappointment of the initially low fee.

Should the subject of copyright be applied to a full-length book, then the publisher will present his offer within a carefully worded contract. Basically, he will propose that, within a specific period of time, he will publish a specific number of books for a specific market, for a specific advance upon royalties. In order to do this, he will purchase only the right to publish your manuscript in book form. He will, however, require an option to negotiate on your behalf all other rights and state clearly the publisher/author percentages involved.

A publishing contract is, even to the well established author, a complicated document, open to misinterpretation by the layman and beyond the reliable understanding of many legal minds. The Society of Authors can provide unparalleled specialist advice on the subject of contracts and once the author has received the contract for signature, he would be well advised to contact the Society to ask for their opinion. On the payment of an annual membership fee, the Society will scrutinise a contract and make a detailed recommendation to the author, covering any points which they feel to be unfavourable. It is then the author's prerogative to approach the publisher with a request that the contract be renegotiated before signature.

If the publisher has reached contract stage, then you may be sure that he genuinely wishes to publish your book and that, whilst you may not be able to reach agreement on all points, he will be open to discussion on many of the points raised in order to secure your agreement.

Start as you mean to go on. With your first submission, begin to keep records. Immediately you begin to enjoy an income, no matter how small from your writing, it is essential to keep a detailed record of both income and expenditure, a subject dealt with in greater depth in Chapter Twelve.

8
WRITING
PICTURE-STRIP

'Tis pleasant, sure, to see one's name in print.
Lord Byron

Whilst much of what has gone before in this book is applicable to writing picture-strip, there are many new rules to be learned if you choose to dip your toe into these particular waters.

To begin with, you must come to terms with the fact that, if your writer's ego needs constantly boosting by seeing your name in print, picture-strip writing is not for you. Whilst you will generally speaking be well paid, in the world of picture-strip writing, the author, in this country at least, remains anonymous.

Rates of payment for picture-strip stories vary according to the publishing house, as with all other forms of writing for children. The technique involved requires a degree of specialised ability, so rates are better, on average, than for text work.

WHO DOES WHAT?

One of the questions often asked by a writer contemplating strip writing is whether they have to draw the pictures as well as write the text. The answer is a straight no.

You are part of a team headed by the editor. It is he who decides which writers and illustrators to use for each strip. Contrary to the beliefs of many, I have never met an editor who did not strive to maintain a good working relationship with his writers. If your aim is to be treated like a professional, then behave like one by considering his priorities. Your initial approach should be by introductory letter, attaching a brief cv of your relevant successes and submitting a full manuscript together with any storylines you may have in synopsis form.

If you have worked for an editor before and have satisfied him that you can produce well crafted script to the required length and in good time for his deadlines, he may well contact you. At this stage, he will ask you to submit a synopsis for an established or new strip character. Once the outline meets with his approval, you will be asked to produce the full manuscript. Although the writing of a synopsis is not the average author's favourite pastime, once you have proved that you have acquired the necessary technique, it saves a great deal of unnecessary work for both the writer and editor should the idea ultimately prove to be a non-starter.

The next stage begins when your manuscript is passed to the artist, without whose talent your character would never achieve graphic life. Remember, he will be working from your written instructions, so clarity is of the utmost importance – but under no circumstances treat him like a fool. Credit him with the commonsense and creativity that he is due. It is important for you to outline both the backdrop and the characters necessary to each frame of the story but do not dot all the i's or cross all the t's. Allow him the artistic freedom to bring your story to life.

The majority of comics nowadays contain full-colour and this is where the colourist will take over the process, bringing the page to new life with all the skill at his fingertips. When you finally see your story in print you will, I hope, appreciate the hours of painstaking work and expert interpretation that went into drawing each frame of your story.

Many picture-strip stories, particularly for the teenage market, are produced in photo strip rather than drawn strip and this requires the used of a skilled and specialist photographer. Your instructions to the photographer will differ only slightly from those you would offer to the artist, although you will be forced to bear in mind the limitations of the camera, when compared with those of the pen. Where an artist is able to recreate a jet liner crashing on a stately home, should the story require such drama, it is unlikely that the editor of a comic would have a budget sufficient to pay for the repairs were he to send a photographer out to capture such a scene.

As most photo strip stories feature girls or boys between the ages of ten and sixteen, the models are usually drawn from local schools, youth clubs or the like and carefully costumed and rehearsed before each shot is taken.

Once the editor is satisfied with the artist's or photographer's work, he will pass the drawn page onto the letterer, whose job it is to reproduce your characters' dialogue in word-bubble form. Once again, this is a highly skilled job, for each word-bubble must be placed in such a way that it does not obscure the action contained within each picture. He will choose not only the size but the shape of the bubble, sometimes giving it a jagged edge to emphasise the content or on a string of tiny bubbles, positioned above the character's head to denote thought rather than dialogue.

Your job as the author, however, is to present the story in such a manner that it will include brief but accurate instructions to the artist or photographer, together with either the relevant caption or a series of word-bubbles and panels.

There is a high degree of satisfaction in seeing your carefully constructed characters and plot come to life, although it can on occasions be a bumpy road. A critical editor may edit your copy until it is barely recognisable, leaving you wondering why they were so precise in their original brief. Another will OK your synopsis and leave you alone to deliver the full manuscript in your own style, changing very little of it before sending it on to the illustrator.

Editors come in many shapes and sizes but the one factor they share is power. Their hand may mutilate your copy but it will also sign the all-important instruction to the accounts department to send you your cheque. The editor knows what makes his particular magazine sell week after week and if you want a place on his team, then take his advice. Whatever happens along the way, you will eventually see your words translated into pictures.

THE HISTORY OF PICTURE-STRIP

Possibly the best way for a would-be strip writer to understand the techniques required for this specialised field is to look back into its history. The comic strip can perhaps best be defined as a sequence of pictures which tell a story with or without the aid of words. It can, some assert, be traced back to cave drawings or Egyptian tomb murals, when our ancestors recorded the events and triumphs of their everyday lives. Certainly, the Bayeux Tapestry is an example of picture-strip. Perhaps it is fair to say, however, that the origins of illustrated text for children, the basis of today's picture-strip, can be traced no further back than the middle of the nineteenth century.

Newspapers as long ago as the 1800s, carried single picture cartoons, usually depicting political comment or one-liner humour, which for many years enjoyed an enthusiastic readership. In 1841, the first edition of *Punch* offered a wider, often satirical, scope for illustrated humour; its success was followed in 1861 by *Fun* and six years later by *Judy*.

English writer and engraver, Edwin John Brett, produced the first of the *Penny Dreadfuls*, full-length stories in weekly episodes. The content, a mixture of crime and cruelty, met with public outrage and by 1866, due to pressure of public opinion, he had cleaned up his act and began to publish a range of good, clean adventure magazines, such as *The Boys of England*, a weekly edition which lasted in popularity for over thirty years. Later, in 1868, Brett was to publish the first comic strip in an English children's periodical, featuring the characters *Long* and *Short*.

The first comic paper produced in a similar format to today's publications was *Funny Folks*, by the Victorian publisher James Henderson in 1874. For the sum of one penny, the reader could enjoy eight pages of laughter, yet still the artist relied upon single picture cartoon humour for adults.

By 1890, *Snapshots* had joined the ranks, reprinting material from several of the American magazines of the time, rapidly followed by another volume of reprints under the title *Comic Cuts*. Marketed at half the price of its competitors, the new publication found instant popularity and, a few months later, *Illustrated Chips* was born out of the same stable.

By 1891, the word 'comic' was firmly established in the mind of the reading public. At first, the text accompanying the pictures was in caption form only, but by 1901 the speech bubble was in use enabling writers and illustrators to move the story forward with dialogue as well as captions.

Young readers grew fond of the characters who debunked the pompous, used native cunning to succeed and became involved in slapstick violence, in which no one was hurt, very much as they do today.

Publishers at the turn of the century, appreciative of the interest shown in children's comics, began to produce a variety of titles. *Rainbow*, which boasted a peak circulation of a million copies, made its appearance at the beginning of the First World War, followed during the 1920s by *Chicks Own*, *Playbox* and *Tiger Tim's Weekly*.

During the following years, the single picture cartoon gave way to sets of pictures depicting humour in action. *Weary Willie* and *Tired Tim*, the tramps who survived from 1896 until 1953, made their debut in a series of weekly picture-strip adventures between the pages of *Chips*. The combination of well drawn sets of pictures and their humorous appeal to a wide age group, coupled with advances in education, brought about the birth of weekly comics aimed specifically at children. As illustrators extended their talents to the comic strip, a sequence of pictures, they discovered a new dimension for expression.

Across the water in the USA, however, it took some time before the potential of comics was fully realised and the world was forced to wait until around 1930 for the advent of such characters as Flash Gordon and his serialised space adventures. An abortive attempt was made in 1929 to launch the first comic paper, containing full-colour picture strips. It was not a notable success but the idea had been born. A few years later a smaller format caught the imagination of the public and attracted the interest of the publishing world. From a mass of experimental characters emerged Jungle Jim, Agent X9 and Fearless Fosdick. The super hero was firmly established in the American home.

These were the forerunners of the comics that we know and love today but perhaps the best place to begin explaining the technique of picture story writing is by examining the simple storyline for pre-school age children, containing a minimum of characters and a single plot accompanied by a clearly worded caption.

Ask your local newsagent which comics are regularly ordered for the pre-school age group, buy a few and settle down to some genuine market research. You will soon realise that the pages between the covers of the pre-school comic are peopled by anthropomorphised animals, toys, witches, wizards and pleasant little visitors from outer space. Even in today's high-tech world, a sprinkling of wee folk, fairies, elves and sprites have still managed to survive.

THE AUDIO VISUAL TEST

Picture-strip stories can bring wonderful characters to life, but the technique involved has to be precise. Imagine for a moment, a busy young mother with a small child waving a comic and asking for it to be read. In a perfect world, every mother would behave as if she were auditioning for Mother of the Year, drop everything with a beatific smile, pull the child lovingly onto her knee and begin to read.

But mothers lead busy lives and the response would be more likely to be, 'Not now, sweetheart, I'm getting dinner' or doing any one of a million other daily tasks.

The child, under these circumstances, will have to be satisfied with looking at the picture strip story and it must, therefore, if he is to understand it, carry the story clearly in picture form alone. He may well be forced to wait until bedtime for the story actually to be read aloud to him when, once Mum or Dad has tucked him up, they will urge him to close his eyes and cuddle down. So positioned, the young listener may not be able to see the pictures. The captions, therefore, must run smoothly together, as in a text story, telling the complete tale in a satisfactory manner of their own.

The ultimate pleasure for the child is when the parent can

set aside some quality time to read aloud the captions and encourage the youngster to point out the events in the accompanying pictures.

Clearly, then, the picture-strip must work on three levels for the pre-school age group. The story told in pictures alone, the read-aloud element smoothly told to interest the child without visual aids, and finally the magic mix of words and pictures brought satisfactorily together.

No matter who you are writing for, the first thing you will need before putting pen to paper is an idea. And remember, the character you may have chosen has possibly appeared in the comic for several years, so it is up to you to find something original in the way of a storyline.

Begin by knowing your character's strengths and weeknesses. An animated toy, a small animal or even one of the little folk, when inhabiting the world of humans will encounter some very real problems.

It is quite logical to the pre-school child for characters such as this to be identified and to interact with young children which, hopefully, will lead to the beginning of exciting adventures or the solution to a variety of problems.

One of the major problems your character may face is size, particularly in relation to everyday objects around them. If, for example, you are writing about an average sized doll, she will have difficulty in moving heavy objects or reaching a high shelf without help.

When writing for this age group, select a suitable toy and keep it clearly in view as you work. Anyone who has actually seen a fairy will, of course, know that they are about two inches high, while elves exceed that measurement by about half an inch. Fish swim, birds and fairies can fly but all other creatures, with one or two exceptions such as Dumbo, have to live their lives with their feet on the ground. Try changing this order of things at your peril. To the young reader, these facts are not open to dispute.

Once you have read as many comics for this age group as you can find, you will realise that much of the material used is very brief and completely uncomplicated. Most of the stories have only six to eight frames or pictures to a page. It is, therefore, necessary to involve your reader in a minimum number of characters and only one simple plot.

Many established characters are literally 'up for grabs'. While the copyright on the character itself often belongs, or is under licence, to the publishing house, the editor still needs storylines for it week after week from capable freelance writers.

By thoroughly familiarising yourself with an established character in one specific magazine over a period of weeks or even months, it will soon become obvious just what will meet with editorial approval. The main character will have a supporting cast of friends which, in themselves, may well suggest to you a variety of additional storylines. I have, for many years, produced scripts for D.C. Thomson. They are a caring publishing house, who help and encourage both new and established writers in the difficult skills required when writing for children.

You will find that the central character in each story inhabits its own setting, a farm, a house or toy cupboard. An example to illustrate this point is *Elfie*. A firm and long established favourite in D.C. Thomson's *Twinkle*, a comic which has been popular with small children since 1968.

Elfie first appeared in *Twinkle* in March 1979, having moved from *Magic*. During the first half of the 1980s, the little fellow lived unseen and unsuspected by all but Poochie, a shaggy dog, in a doll's house in the home of a small girl called Mary. His adventures, needs and desires were prompted by the world he saw in Mary's home, on television, or perhaps Poochie would smuggle him out in his long fur, maybe on a family outing.

The ingenuity of the author was to utilise a thimble as a pot for a tiny plant in the doll's house or an old woollen glove, suitably tailored as warm socks, gloves and hat for the little elf. He is on good terms with garden and sea birds and often finds them a useful alternative to British Airways when the author wishes a new backdrop for a story.

He communes with rabbits and other small creatures but never with humans. Any visible evidence of Elfie's adventures is always put down to 'the special magic'.

Then in 1986 Mary, her family, dolls' house and all, moved, leaving Elfie behind. Of necessity, he took to the woods and for two years, his adventures took place in the company of an assortment of other wee folk until, in November 1988, after helping the Fairy Queen, he was granted a wish to return to live again with Mary.

The series continued within Mary's home, until July 1989 then, after a short absence from *Twinkle*, Elfie reappeared in a story which took him outside to be blown away in a kite and rescued by Poochie. He was once again reunited with Mary and the series continued in her home until April 1990.

A brand new series, which ran for three months only, began in August 1990 with Elfie and Poochie teaming up with Sylvester, a black Siamese cat, who they meet in a holiday cottage, while another Elfie story ran from January to May 1991 with Elfie back in the woods rescuing an elfish princess from an ice wizard.

SCRIPT LAYOUT

Analysing an example of a complete picture strip story for this character will illustrate the boundaries within which the author must work. For example, a two-page story for this character, when examined frame by frame covers a total of nine pictures and captions, the first of which is the standard title beginning to any Elfie story. Its function is briefly to introduce the character to the child and requires no work on the part of the writer.

The story really begins in the second frame, setting the scene inside Mary's house where her cousin has come to play, bringing with him some building blocks and a toy car. If you look closely at the illustration (Figure 1) the artist has, at the writer's request, shown the little elf looking out from the window of his home, Mary's dolls' house. The caption beneath the picture tells the first part of the story in an economical nineteen words.

The editor has chosen to show the third picture as a colouring and puzzle exercise for the young reader. The caption on the left continues to tell the tale, while on the

© D.C. Thomson & Co. Ltd.

Elfie is a tiny elf who lives secretly in Mary's doll's house
When he makes things happen, Mary thinks it is magic
Poochie, Mary's big dog, is Elfie's best friend.

1 — Mary's cousin, Peter, came to
play one day. He brought a box of
bricks and his shiny, new car.

2 — Mary and Peter played in the playroom "It
would be nice if my doll's house had a garage,"
Mary said. "Ooh, yes!" thought Elfie.

You can colour this picture, using your paints or
crayons. There are six sponges hidden in the
picture. Can you see them?

Figure 1 *Extract from D.C. Thomson's Twinkle Comic*

3 — Peter also agreed with Mary. "It's just what the house needs," he said. "Let's build it after tea." "All right," said Mary, happily.

4 — Just then, Mummy looked into the playroom. "Time for tea!" she called. "Oh, good!" cried Mary and Peter. "We're *starving!*"

5 — When they had gone, Elfie thought, "I think I'll build the garage. I've always wanted to be a builder." Poochie helped his chum.

6 — Elfie worked very hard. He was just driving the car into the garage, when Mary and Peter came back. "That was close!" Elfie gasped.

7 — Mary and Peter were surprised to see the garage. "It's super," said Peter. "It's just the right size for my car too!"

8 — "But who could have built the garage?" puzzled Peter. "I know," said Mary, with a smile. "It was the special magic at work again!"

Figure 2 *Extract from D.C. Thomson's Twinkle Comic*

right, the child is asked to search the picture for six hidden sponges.

Frames three to eight, shown in the next illustration, (Figure 2) carry the remainder of the story through from Mary's desire to build a garage for the toy car alongside the doll's house to the children's disappearance when they are called for their tea. Here Elfie, who has been seen watching closely throughout, takes over the action. Under the watchful eye and with the help of his pal, Poochie the dog, he builds the garage. He just has time to drive the little car under cover and to hide, when the children return. They are delighted but puzzled. Mary, however, knows it is just the 'special magic' at work again.

The finished manuscript originally sent to *Twinkle*'s editor looked like this (with Pic being an abbreviation for Picture, and Cap for Caption):

Pic 1:   Mary's cousin Peter arrives at her house to play. He carries a box of bricks and a toy car. Elfie seen looking through window of doll's house.

Cap 1:   Mary's cousin, Peter, came to play one day. He brought a box of bricks and his shiny car.

Pic 2:   Mary playing with doll's house, Peter crawling along with car nearby. Bricks out of box in pile on the floor. Elfie seen watching at edge of frame.

Cap 2:   Mary and Peter played in the playroom. 'It would be nice if my doll's house had a garage.' Mary said, 'Ooh yes!' thought Elfie.

Pic 3:   Close-up of Mary and Peter talking. Doll's house and bricks in background.

Cap 3:   Peter also agreed with Mary, 'It's just what the house needs,' he said, 'let's build it after tea.' 'All right,' said Mary, happily.

Pic 4:   Mummy's head appears round door and Mary and Peter are called away to tea. Elfie watches them go.

Cap 4:   Just then, mummy looked into the playroom, 'time for tea!' she called. 'Oh good!' cried Mary and Peter, 'we're starving.'

111

Pic 5:   Poochie is carrying bricks over to the doll's house in his mouth while Elfie works on the garage, which is more than half built.

Cap 5:   When they had gone, Elfie thought, 'I think I'll build the garage. I've always wanted to be a builder.' Poochie helped his chum.

Pic 6:   Elfie driving the car into finished garage as the two children walk in the door.

Cap 6:   Elfie worked very hard. He was just driving the car into the garage when Mary and Peter came back. 'That was close!' Elfie gasped.

Pic 7:   Mary on knees looking thrilled at garage, Peter looks puzzled – he scratches his head. Elfie laughing behind corner of house.

Cap 7:   Mary and Peter were surprised to see the garage. 'It's super,' said Peter, 'It's just the right size for my car, too!'

Pic 8:   Peter proudly pushing his car in an out of the garage, Mary looking pleased.

Cap 8:   'But who could have built the garage?' puzzled Peter. 'I know,' said Mary, with a smile, 'It was the special magic at work again.'

To the adult mind, the idea of an elf living in a doll's house, building a garage and driving a toy car is, to say the least, a little unlikely. But to the mind of the very young child, all things are possible. This is due to the strength built into the character in question.

Every young devotee of this particular strip knows that Elfie is kind, generous, fun loving and ingenious. While he was living in the doll's house, they accepted that it was fully equipped for his needs, including a complete set of tools and an elf-sized sewing machine.

Before reading any further, try the audio visual test. First look at the pictures without the benefit of the text to establish whether the young mind would understand the storyline in picture form alone. Then read the text without the benefit of the pictures and you will see that it clearly stands on its own.

8–TEENS

In comics and magazines for older children, there is far more scope for both humour and adventure serials. Comics like *The Dandy* and *The Beano*, both from the publishing house of D.C. Thomson, shot to instant popularity in the 1930s golden age of comics and are still widely read and enjoyed today. Generation after generation remembers with affection the antics of *Desperate Dan*, *Korky the Kat* and *Keyhole Kate* but changing attitudes of the 90s have taken their toll. *Lord Snooty and His Pals* was recently dropped due to the belief that today's reader could no longer identify with the characters and *Desperate Dan's* dietary obsession with cow pie has come under the disapproving eye of the vegetarian lobby.

Over the span of years, a variety of illustrators have added their talents towards the perfection of the picture-strip technique, improving the sense of movement within the picture, using close-ups to show expression on the face of the character, and limiting the amount of text. Word-bubbles have taken on a new importance and frames of varying shapes and sizes have added interest to the general appearance of the page.

When the well drawn full-colour *Eagle* took flight in the 50s, its spirited and imaginative adventure stories soared to instant popularity with both children and parents. Within two years, the equally professional *Lion* was enjoying the same success and the same year saw the launch of a range of comics for girls, geared specifically for their own interests. Publications such as *Bunty* and *Judy* were filled with picture-strip serial, featuring tales of mystery and adventure, ballet and horse riding.

VISUALISATION

There is enormous scope within the pages of these comics not only for new storylines for established characters but also for good, well written original serials.

One tried and tested way of working is to take an A4 lined pad and working from your original synopsis, visualise the tale episode by episode. Then outline the entry and exit of the

113

main characters and include one major occurrence and a cliffhanger ending for each weekly episode.

Number the margin with the requisite amount of frames, leaving eight or nine lines between each figure, and spread the action equally between them, instructing the artist or if the story is destined to appear in photo strip, the photographer, exactly who and what you wish to appear in each picture or frame.

It may be necessary to show on the face of one of the characters the emotional impact caused by words spoken by a companion. Instructions to the illustrator should be along the following lines:

Pic 1:   An outdoor running track. Wendy Miller and Sandra Smyth, her rival, are running neck and neck. Wendy's friend, Janet can be seen watching and cheering on far right. She has a stopwatch in her hand.
      Leave space for dialogue here.

Pic 2:   Wendy has crossed the line ahead of her rival and is being congratulated by Janet. Sandra has crossed the line seconds after her and looks furious. She points a finger accusingly at Wendy.
      Leave space for dialogue here.

Pic 3:   Changing room. Wendy changing and talking to Janet. Sandra with one of her cronies can be seen at far end of changing room.
      Leave space for dialogue here.

Pic 4:   Same background but close-up of Janet and Wendy who is happily waving a four leaf clover contained in an open locket on a chain.
      Leave space for dialogue here.

DIALOGUE

The dialogue must exactly match the action in each frame you have outlined to this illustrator. Using the frame outlined above, the dialogue would be set out as follows:

Pic 1:   (Instructions to artist as above)
Janet: 'Come on, Wendy, you can beat her, just a few more yards.'
Pic 2:   (Instructions to artist as above)
Sandra: 'You fouled me. You deliberately changed lanes.'
Janet: 'Rubbish! Wendy doesn't have to cheat to win. The Carrington Trophy is as good as hers.'
Pic 3:   (Instructions to artist as above)
Panel: Later in the changing room
Janet: 'That was your best time yet. You're sure to beat Sandra on Saturday.'
Wendy: 'I'm not taking any chances. I'm keeping my fingers crossed.'
Pic 4:   (Instructions to artist as above)
Janet: 'Not more of that superstitious rubbish! You'll win because you're the fastest runner.'
Wendy: 'Believe what you like but my lucky clover goes wherever I go.';

Once both the instructions to the artist and the dialogue have been completed, you have a first draft from which to work.

As with a full length novel, characterisation is all important. Create your central characters with enough conviction and the story will appear to write itself, fail to do so and it will grind to a halt. Here you are working not only with words but with pictures, something you will come to realise gives you much more scope. But it is a facet which you may find difficult to cope with at first, for in the past you have been confined to showing not telling, using words alone to create pictures in the mind of your reader. It could take several rewrites before you are satisfied and ready to submit your manuscript to an editor.

INSTRUCTIONS TO THE ARTISTS

In publications for older children the story is carried forward by dialogue alone, with an occasionally explanatory panel taking the reader forward in time or from one location to another.

When writing your manuscript, bear in mind the problems you may create at this stage. Whilst it is possible for the artist to fit perhaps five characters into a single picture, should they all decide to speak at once and at length, it is going to be extremely difficult for five word-bubbles to be included in that frame without obliterating the artist's hard work. Bear in mind too, the nature of the utterance. As you can see from the illustration taken from the D.C. Thomson comic *Mandy and Judy* in Figure 3, the word-bubble has been carefully positioned so as not to obscure the faces or hands of the two characters. Figure 4 contains an explosive phrase which, to give the necessary impact, appears within a shape that has a jagged edge, whilst Figure 5, taken from the same story, illustrates how a thought-bubble will hover, as if on a string of soap suds, above the head of the character.

Many publishers use illustrators native to countries other than Great Britain. Consequently, misunderstandings can arise due to the vagaries of our language. There is a beautiful, and one is lead to believe true, story about the writer who issued instructions to his illustrator that one of the characters in the tale was a 'chinless wonder' standing in front of a 'one-armed bandit'. The result was hardly what the writer had in mind, so make a mental note now that it pays to be explicit and to avoid slang terms.

© D.C. Thomson & Co. Ltd.

Figure 3 *A carefully positioned word bubble*

Figure 4 *A jagged edge showing angry words*

Figure 5 *Tiny bubbles depicting thought rather dialogue*

THE COMIC TODAY

Since their heyday in the 30s, the popularity of comics has plummeted dramatically. The fall-off, at its worst in the 70s was, many believe, largely due to the advent of video games and other pocket-money consuming ideas on the toy market. The good news, however, is that once again, there are signs that the comic has a firm footing on the newsagents' shelves and in its appeal to the young reader.

A percentage of this revival is due to the altered nature of many of the publications in question. There is, for example, a whole new area of interest promoted by children's television programmes and cartoons. Toy manufacturers, too, have played their part by producing appealing characters in the form of a doll, action figure or soft toy that has caught the imagination of the child. Extensive planning accompanies the introduction of such a character and will include, at its launch, not only a series of animated cartoons suitable for television but also, in many cases, an accompanying comic, either as a weekly on the newsagents' stands or as a giveaway in the product pack.

Many well known and much loved characters, such as the *Care Bears* and *My Little Pony* have their own comics which enjoy a regular and devoted readership among the very young. For older girls, the long established *Barbie* and *Princess She-Ra* continue to hold market interest through picture-strip. Characters such as *Thundercats* and *He-Man* are much sought after by boys of a similar age, and once again offer enjoyment by living out their fantasy adventures in picture-strip form.

The majority of these comics are for the younger reader who is still happy to indulge in the magic world of fantasy, but as the child emerges into the vital years between nine and thirteen, he becomes thirsty for more down to earth action set against a background of realism to which he can relate.

It is interesting to note that the pendulum appears to be swinging back to old values. A few years ago, in a bid no doubt for increased sales on the part of the publishing house, many of the comics for this age group which, at the time, won approval from reader and parent alike, were suddenly revamped. A new brand of realism appeared and subjects previously considered taboo were often found within the basic storyline. Many of the comics, quite literally, went 'pop', cramming the pages with coloured photographs of pop music idols; their letters pages and opinion columns were filled with advice on fashion, make-up and dating techniques.

For a while, the publishers enjoyed the fruits of the undeniable surge of renewed interest. An interest which, however, has shown a decline in the intervening years. The publishers have been forced to acknowledge that, generally speaking, the subject matter on offer was perhaps a little too mature for the age group at which it was aimed. Many of these publications are now slowly returning to their original format of good, clean humour and adventure.

Those titles which did not succumb to the revamping rush of publisher enthusiasm have survived. Throughout the period they have continued successfully to run the standard schoolgirl/schoolboy adventure story. Perhaps the best recent example of this re-emergence can be found in the enduring comic *Eagle*, and its treatment of clean-cut 50s space pilot hero Dan Dare.

For more than twenty years, Dan Dare has been banished from *Eagle's* prime front page slot to pursue his adventures in a far less prestigious position inside the comic. Recently, however, he was promoted back to the starring front role by popular request of the readership. Seen as an antidote to today's sophisticated high-tech characters, Dan's only concession to the 90s is a romance with secondary character Professor Jocelyn Peabody. Even arch-villain and long standing adversary The Mekon is still determined to conquer the Earth while typically British Dan Dare looks set to defend our planet well into the 21st century.

CREATING NEW CHARACTERS

Dan Dare is of course well established, as are many other characters in the pages of the wide variety of comics available today. In almost every case, as with some of the pre and

119

primary school publications, the copyright on the character in question is owned by the publishing house, most of whom will welcome new writers who can prove that they can produce new and exciting storylines.

It is well worthwhile approaching an editor by telephone or by letter to establish whether or not he would be prepared to consider the work of a new writer. You must, of course, have acquired the necessary technique and be prepared to prove your point by supplying for his approval a completed manuscript in the correct format. He will be more likely to welcome you into his team if you can accompany such a manuscript with half a dozen or more additional storylines in synopsis form. This will prove to him that you have a thorough knowledge of the character and are not a one-off contributor.

It may be that you have a brilliant idea for a central figure for which you can supply dozens of storylines. If the editor feels it has the right appeal and the potential to become established over a reasonable length of time, he will of course wish to purchase it. Bear in mind, however, that should this be his intention, he will buy the copyright on the character, along with your original storylines. You, the originator, once having agreed to the sale, will have no further income from the character in the form of subsidiary rights should it subsequently become a moneyspinner in the toy or television world.

In an offer to purchase, the phrase 'All Rights For All Purposes' is not necessarily one to be avoided. But it is one to be approached with caution: in exchange for a one-off and often modest payment, you will be parting with what amounts to your complete copyright.

As I mentioned in the previous chapter, there are many examples of authors parting with the rights to characters who subsequently became household names and possible the most famous of these is the story of Superman.

Superman had been turned down by a number of publishers so, in 1938 when the offer from *Detective Comics* came along, Joe Shuster and Jerry Siegel had no hesitation in selling all rights to their creation for the princely sum of £75.

Only when Superman appeared on film in serial form

some ten years later did they attempt to sue *Detective Comics* – with the result that they were fired and new illustrators and writers brought in to take over the character.

Not until 1975, when Warner Bros made the first Superman film and were ordered by the courts to give Shuster and Siegel 'financial recognition' did they earn anything from their creation. After years of poverty, during which the Superman character earned millions of pounds, his originators finally received an annual pension of £10,000.

As explained at the start of this chapter, avoid the world of strip-writing if you long to see your name in print. If, however, you are seeking an accessible, thorough and highly enjoyable training in the technique and disciplines of your craft, then strip-writing is for you.

9
SPECIFIC SPECIALIST MARKETS

A young branch takes on all the bends that one gives it.
Chinese Proverb

The appeal of pictures to the young child is undeniable. Parents actively encourage the pre-school child to read and increase his vocabulary, using the most simple of picture books to assist progress. As a story is read, the young listener will eagerly point out the illustrated characters and situations relevant to the text as the pages are turned, so becoming totally involved in the tale. At a later stage, left alone with the same book, the new reader will identify the written word by using the pictures to help him through the story.

Picture books become favourites, familiar bedtime comforters and are passed on from one child in the family to the next, often surviving even the gap between generations. You have only to watch the young mother in a library smilingly select for her child a well remembered volume of Dr Seuss or Beatrix Potter to see the truth of this statement.

The alphabet book, A is for Apple, B is for Ball, is a bookshelf priority for the under fives, usually accompanied by a volume of brightly coloured nursery rhymes. Indeed in generations gone by, these, together with a few classics and a handful of Bible storybooks, constituted the whole of what was quite a small area of the overall children's book market.

One of the earliest recorded books for children is a collection of Aesop's Fables published in 1585 but it was not until the early 18th century that the printer John Newbury produced books specifically for children.

There are picture books covering a wide range of non-fiction subjects and in a comprehensive collection of children's books spanning the generations may be found Victorian moral tales sitting uneasily alongside books like *Jenny Lives with Eric and Martin*. There has always been a wealth of pop-up and interactivity books which can be either intricately detailed or bright and clear depending upon the fashion of the day, while the outstandingly original illustrations of authors such as Maurice Sendak in his wonderful *Where The Wild Things Are* have lifted them into the realm of the modern classic.

You have only to browse along the shelves of a bookshop to realise that the picture book is enjoying the popularity it has always deserved. Editors are constantly looking for those qualities needed in a writer to produce this unique form of reading matter, and to acquire those qualities it is imperative for you to be able to recall even the most minute details of your own childhood.

THE DEVELOPING CHILD

When remembering your early years you will need, above all, a visual sense. This may at first seem to be impossible, but with a little concentrated thought it can be achieved.

Peel back the layers of your memory one by one, stretching your powers of recall, unearthing people and instances which have lain untouched for years. Family photos are often of enormous help in this exercise. A creased and dog-eared black and white snap of myself as a toddler sitting on the knee of my grandfather evokes memories of the smell of pipe tobacco and the tiny tell-tale burns on his cardigan front, slippers flattened at the heel for comfort, shoulder shaking near silent chuckles at my constant and innocent questions, and the way his spectacles slipped from his nose when he fell asleep over a book.

With only a little persuasion my own father's pronounced Essex drawl still echoes in my memory. I can not only see but feel again the ugly scar on the third finger of his left hand where an injury from a carelessly wielded axe healed badly. I remember too his obsession with personal hygiene which began in the cold water trough on the farm where he was born and remained with him to the end of his life.

The smiling man who in my early years spelled security, and who towered above me, became my friend as I grew and somewhere along the way, I watched him grow old, delighting in the quiet years in the company of my mother and my own children. He would sit in an enormous leather club armchair with a small child perched on either arm, my daughter's tiny fingers entwined in his thinning fair hair, my son's head on his shoulder, as he read yet again from one of their favourite picture books. I can see him still, clearly in my mind's eye, not gone, merely tucked away in memory's labyrinth and on many occasions some facet of his personality has taken its place within the grandfather character in a children's story.

The most successful authors clearly exhibit the ability to write as a child rather than for the child, weaving into the text a special insight encompassing the basic logic, limited experience and unencumbered imagination of the reader.

WHO ILLUSTRATES THE PICTURE BOOK?

It would be wrong to assume that illustrations in a picture book, no matter how beautiful, will give the necessary life to a poor story. The text must be of sufficient quality to inspire both publisher and illustrator before the first step towards publication occurs.

Similarly, an unimaginatively illustrated book, no matter how good the text, will not take and hold the interest of the non-reading child. A good picture book is, therefore, the end product of the interaction between author and illustrator.

Many of the best loved picture books available in today's bookshops are the work of author-illustrators, many of whom began as purely illustrators in their own right. If you have definite illustrative skills and feel that you can supply an editor with high quality illustrations to accompany your text, then you are indeed among the most fortunate in this field.

An excellent example of a successful author-illustrator is Rodney Peppe, whose detailed drawings have delighted children for many years and whose Huxley Pig character regularly appears in animated form on our television screens.

The finely drawn pictures depicting Phoebe Worthington's Teddy Bear friends can also be seen to contain intricate detail which delights and guides the child's eye through the pictures, thereby skilfully increasing his enjoyment of the story, which she lays out in caption form beneath each illustration.

Should you possess the necessary artistic skills, you should send, together with the text, all or at least several of your illustrations to the editor for approval. But do not be disappointed if, ultimately, he accepts only your text and commissions another artist to furnish the illustrations.

If you are unsure of your illustrative capabilities but still wish to present a fully illustrated manuscript to a prospective publisher, then there is an alternative open to you: to collaborate from the outset with an artist of your choice. It may be that a member of your family or circle of friends feels equal to the task but, before you risk making a lifelong enemy by inviting them to illustrate your work, be very sure that the standard of the finished illustrations is likely to stand a chance of acceptance. Not only will they need to be a proficient artist but they will have to work with you to bring to visual life the concept which is wholly and originally yours.

At the end of the day, it may be that whilst the publisher may accept your text, he may reject the illustrations and this should be made quite clear before any collaborating artist embarks upon the project.

It may be necessary for you to look further afield for an illustrator and many young artists have found their way into the book world following their final exams at art college, when their work has been displayed to the public. On such an occasion, the author can discover a wealth of talent eager to find its niche and it may well be that a profitable partnership will ensue.

Simplicity for the pre and primary school market is of paramount importance and, to your adult mind, many picture books may lack what you would define as a storyline. Most, however, have a logical progression or theme leading the child from the first to the last page in a satisfying and informative manner. The techniques, therefore, differ from that of picture-strip writing in several ways, usually relying far more heavily on the interpretative skills of the illustrator.

A good publisher will have a stable of artists upon whom he can rely to produce illustrations for well written texts. Should he feel your manuscript has sufficient possibilities, he will provide a suitable illustrator for your original idea.

POPULAR PICTURE BOOKS

Here, once again, you must do your own market research in bookshops, schools and local libraries. Bookshops exist to make a profit; the choice of material for their shelves is therefore of prime importance to the bookseller. No matter how persuasive the representative's sales talk, the successful businessman will use his own judgement based on daily contact with children and parents before placing his order. Ask his advice, his is the finger unerringly on the day to day pulse of opinion. It is worth bearing in mind, as does he, that the publisher must produce a book worthy of the approval of the adult and it is the parent or relative who makes the all-important purchase.

Again, I suggest that you visit schools, making an appointment to talk to the teacher in charge of buying books for the school library. This teacher's task is to select books which offer maximum enjoyment while at the same time stretching the imagination and capabilities of young minds. The choice will usually range from story picture books to the first steps in science and history. The seeds of many interests and hobbies are planted in these early years, and teachers will do their best to obtain books which outline the basis of collecting, birdwatching, animal care, handicrafts and art.

Librarians, too, are in the privileged position of daily contact with opinion and they are perhaps the keenest critics. They will select titles from the publisher's lists which they feel sure will be well received by the reader. Listen to what they say; they are in an excellent position to judge current trends and requirements. In the course of their day they become aware that adult tastes do not always coincide with those of the young reader, many books which may cause an initial frown of mild disapproval from Mum or Dad will, some might think inexplicably, find popularity with the child who can relate to the naughty or foolish behaviour of the central character. They know that for this age group the book will very often be read aloud by an adult or older child.

In one local library, among the picture books most often selected are those by the award winning Janet and Alan Ahlberg, Pat Hutchins, Shirley Hughes and of course Eric Hill's *Spot the Dog* books. It is interesting to note, however, that according to this children's librarian, children do not select their own books until the age of four. Although they will make their preference known by their enthusiasm, or lack of it, for a particular book, initially the appeal of the illustrations will almost certainly have been to the parent accompanying the child.

It is, nevertheless, the child who makes the final selection and will decide whether your picture book is destined to gather dust on the shelf or become an award winning bestseller. There may be a point during your research when you feel that there are currently far too many picture books on the market. You may feel that your best ideas have already been done to death. Wrong again, don't despair. In an ideal world, the tastes and interests of every child should and would be catered for and publishers as yet have not achieved this perfection.

The pre and primary school child is therefore well catered for in both the world of books and comics, but we have already examined the age-blurring factor when attempting to outline the age groups.

EXPANSION OF HORIZONS

It is usual however, for the child to have begun the process of learning to read by the age of six, individual ability thereafter determining the speed of progress. Interest areas, humour appreciation and the use of vocabulary however, by this time, have broadened considerably. For the six to eight year old child who can still legitimately ask that he be read to aloud, this wider comprehension allows entry into a whole new world of adventure.

Real stories of around 300 to 800 words with simple plots designed to hold the attention, and characters drawn from life or the writer's imagination serve to coax the reader on into the realms of fiction.

For young readers apart from the range of weekly and monthly comics and juvenile magazines there is also a variety of publications related to specialist interests. Cub Scouts and Brownies both publish their own journals. Sunday School or church-based groups, here and abroad, have a wide range of suitable material on offer. Eager young ornithologists and collectors can order relevant publications from their newsagent, or by subscription, as can pony owners and budding sportsmen.

The majority of comics, however, are more general in their content, offering a mix of text and picture-strip stories, 'how to do' features, puzzles and competitions. Compare the comic for the six to eight year old with that published for the pre-school child and the differences between the two will become immediately apparent.

Many of the books on offer for these first time readers fall into the 'series' category, spanning both fact and fiction in a manner which may easily be assimilated by the young mind.

There is a sense of wonder to be enjoyed by anyone privileged to watch a child grow, both physically and emotionally, to maturity. But think back if you can to your own budding years: you may begin to remember some of the agonising mountains which only now, with adult hindsight, can at long last be reduced to molehills.

CONFLICTING EMOTIONS

An excellent publication entitled *Dear Jo*, by *Early Times* the independent newspaper for young people, highlighted many of the problems which dominate the lives and emotions of the developing child. The book was based on letters written to *Early Times* advise column by children between the ages of five and sixteen. Every letter was answered in an understanding and caring manner by a child psychotherapist. Many of the areas of concern are obvious, and are to be expected as the child leaves the security of its home environment and journeys into a world populated not only by its peers but by new and powerful figures of authority. From this precarious background, comes a fountain of material from which the writer may draw a million storylines.

Friends, or the lack of them, are of enormous importance to the growing child, exhibiting a need to be part of the herd. A child who is different in some way, perhaps born into a rich or into a poor family, may well be considered different and become rejected by its peers. The child from the high-income family may quite unfairly, be considered to be a snob due only to its parents' lifestyle. At the opposite end of the monetary scale, the same rejection could arise from the mere fact that the child's parents cannot afford designer trainer shoes, or the cost of a school outing or holiday.

Children are notoriously cruel to one another and an argument between friends may cause what will seem to the adult mind a disproportionate reaction. Nevertheless many instances of truancy and, sadly, even attempted suicide can be traced to the child's reluctance to face public isolation, bullying or ridicule by its peers.

The agony of unrequited love causes pain from a surprisingly early age. The unwitting object of this innocent desire may of course, be an equally immature member of the opposite sex, perhaps a friend from school or a neighbour. Often, it is of an obsessive nature, centring upon one of the obtainable idols in the pop music world, or a familiar tv soap personality. Girls in particular often develop crushes upon their teachers and many of them are concerned that, as their idol too is female, they may be exhibiting gay tendencies. Whatever the cause, the pain is real and it is a wise parent who will listen, and a wise author who will write his story in such a way that it will reassure the young heart that it is merely learning to love.

Despite the abject despair the young reader may be experiencing, he or she will undoubtedly heal and live to love another day. As the mind of the child matures so does its body. The mysteries of how a baby is conceived and born are easily learned by reading some of the many excellent and informative books on the subject written with this age group in mind. It is a fortunate child however, who can discuss these matters frankly with its parent, or discover an author who has looked beyond the mechanics of reproduction and explains the all-important depth of emotion which accompanies the sexual act. Misleading old wives' tales, which can often be terrifying, still abound among the ill-informed and the need to know the truth is a matter of priority to the young enquiring mind. It may be it is embarrassment on the part of the parent which causes the lack of communication or, perhaps a seemingly ever present younger member of the family constantly 'listening in'.

The range of books available for the child who has mastered the art of reading alone is, thankfully, both wide and enjoyable. The continuing magic of authors such as Dick King-Smith offers not only humour but a subtle parallel between the problems of his animal characters and those of the maturing child.

In his latest book, *The Guard Dog* his character is a scruffy little mongrel dog who shares the petshop window with five posh pedigree puppies. The pup's ambition to become a guard dog in someone's house is the subject of ridicule by his five upper-crust companions.

Many young readers will immediately identify with the 'different from the herd' problem which may beset their own existence. A clear comparison can be seen to be drawn between the puppy and the child. It is worth noting that the author has a personal background, rooted in farm life and later in primary school teaching, from which he has obviously drawn invaluable experience.

Bernard Ashley, however, whilst writing for readers of roughly the same age group, deals caringly with similar problems but in a realistic manner. His experience as a headmaster has enabled him in his book *Your Guess Is As Good As Mine* sensitively to handle the abduction of a child. His characters, who are real children, help the police to find the central character by using their own native intelligence and following the correct path, carefully laid down by the author as a subliminal blueprint for correct procedure in such a situation.

Both of these authors indisputably know how to tell a good tale, but where one uses the animal world as a vehicle for humorous substitution in the cause of education, the other strikes directly at the heart of the problem, pulling no punches in order to educate the child about an all-important issue.

The runaway success of Bantam's American romance series *Sweet Valley High* prompted the publication of a junior version, *Sweet Valley Kids*. The books are designed for a five to nine year old readership and in *Sweet Valley Slumber Party* by Francine Pascal, identical twins Elizabeth and Jessica invite four friends to a slumber party, but things go wrong and the girls argue and fall out.

Once again, despite the obligatory happy ending, the emotions of the growing child are explored and explained in a manner with which they will undoubtedly identify, allowing them to take another small step towards the important goal of human relationships.

THE INFLUENCE OF TELEVISION

Television, which must surely influence to some degree the minds of almost every child in today's world, relaunched the *Thunderbirds* puppet series of adventures several years after the original series. Calculated to be of interest to the seven to nine year old reader, Young Corgi began a series of books based on the amazing exploits of Geoff Tracey and his talented and courageous *Thunderbird* sons.

The television relaunch to a second generation of viewers not only guaranteed the success of the accompanying books but gave rise to a range of new toys sought after by both children and parents (many of whom may have toys from the original series tucked away in an attic or old toybox).

Original *Thunderbird* vehicles and figures became highly collectable as the second generation of books and toys eased themselves into popularity.

BANANA SKIN HUMOUR

Humour as a component part of any story written for this age group is a much sought after commodity by the discerning editor. However, at this stage in their growth, the child's appreciation of humour is without subtlety. The innuendo, parody, pun and satire, all of which appeal to the adult mind, will miss the child's funnybone by a mile. Slapstick, in one form or another is by far the more appealing to the reader, a truth that is well illustrated in many of the comics available today. Generations of children have chortled, and will continue to chortle, when a character slips on a banana skin, is the recipient of a custard pie or gets his comeuppance in one of a variety of unlikely, yet graphic ways.

In the book world, humour within an everyday setting, such as home or school, seems to offer the most enjoyment to the young reader but must be seen through the eyes of the child. Fully to appreciate the wide range of circumstances which will cause a child genuinely to laugh aloud, once again the would-be writer should read everything currently available in the genre.

On the shelves of most school libraries you will find a high percentage of books written in humorous vein, many of them collections of poems. *A Gerbil in the Hoover* by Jerome Fletcher, cleverly illustrated by Nick Sharratt and published by Corgi, is a delightful collection of poems and stories which, seen from the child's viewpoint, cover such material as the problems of being lonely or overweight through to Queen Boadicea shopping in a supermarket. Skunks and maggots are gleefully featured as Ibn Ivri Warmun, the genie who appears in a television rather than the conventional bottle.

Possibly the most sought after books in this genre are from the pens of such names as Roger McGough, Michael Rosen and Kit Wright. They all have the ability not only to see but to wickedly enjoy the type of humour that appeals to the young reader. They appreciate all the awful things that children are forced to endure at the hands of seemingly over-reactive adults. Being slobbered over by enthusiastic relatives when forced to offer that inescapable kiss on the shrivelled cheek of Aunty Flo, having to deal with spiteful siblings, being made to do their share of household chores or tidy up their messy bedrooms are all situations which, to the adult mind, are unimportant – but for the child can dominate their day.

In *Hod Dog and Other Poems* by Kit Wright, illustrated by Posy Simmons and published by Puffin, the reader is introduced to Dave Dirt, who is invited by the family to dinner. It is impossible to read *Dave Dirt Came To Dinner* without laughing, as it expresses the child's glee at the discomfort of the adults concerned:

> Dave Dirt came to dinner
> And he stuck his chewing gum
> Underneath the table
> And it didn't please my Mum
>
> And it didn't please my Granny
> Who was quite a sight to see
> When she got up from the table
> With the gum stuck to her knee
>
> Where she put her cup and saucer
> When she sat and drank her tea
> And the saucer and the chewing gum
> Got stuck as stuck can be
> And she staggered round the kitchen
> With a saucer on her skirt –
> No, it didn't please my Granny
> But it PLEASED DAVE DIRT.

From the adult's point of view Dave Dirt is clearly a highly undesirable character, but as far as the child is concerned he would be welcomed as light relief and the opportunity to challenge authority at any formal tea table.

The subject of humour should not exclude Roald Dahl, overwhelmingly one of the most popular children's authors of today. At one time his humour was accepted by the adult

133

book purchaser, largely due to the demand of the child. Recently, however, schools and parents alike have taken a closer look at his work and concerns are being voiced that Dahl appears to subject adult strictures to ridicule and endorse children's impulses to vengeance and aggression.

Undeniably, his contemporary fantasies appeal to the young reader but adult watchdogs, such as parents and librarians, are beginning to say that the mixture of sadism and black humour contained in his books leaves them feeling uncomfortable.

Shortly before his death, this concern manifested itself in a public controversy over the publication of *Rhyme Stew* a collection of poems which, whilst undeniably amusing, were considered by many to border on the edge of pornography. *A Hand In the Bird* which appears to trivialise sexual assault and *Physical Training* which could be interpreted as the tale of a female teacher sexually abusing a young boy, are two examples of poems which might never have appeared in a book for children had the author not been so highly acclaimed in the literary world.

Much of Roald Dahl's work quite clearly exhibits his own emotional hang-ups and prejudices which may well subliminally influence the young reader in later life. Perhaps, therefor, adult opinion should have the courage to make a stand against authors whose work could damage the emotional health of today's child. They should not be so intimidated by the commercial success of any author whose work causes them concern, neither should they continue to promote anything, no matter how popular it may be, which in their opinion would be harmful or destructive. Humour should be seen to equate with fun and laughter and not be used as a vehicle for spite and hatred.

There can be few children's authors who would not aspire to achieve the success and status of Roald Dahl, but those who seek to emulate his style should proceed with caution. They may well find that, due to public demand, the publishing world is less willing to consider this individual and somewhat unsavoury humour.

The backlash against writers such as Roald Dahl took the

publishing world full circle back to the good old dependable adventure story style of that other pariah of children's fiction, Enid Blyton.

MYSTERY AND ADVENTURE

Child detectives are much in demand, particularly in the world of series books. A good solid mystery for the reader to solve, especially if it is woven through an exciting adventure, still has enormous appeal for the young reader.

Adventures often take the form of ghost stories or science fiction and fantasy novels and there is a huge revival in the popularity of school stories.

Conservation is very much in the forefront of children's education and awareness today and publishers are always on the lookout for good, strong stories dealing with environmental issues, animal welfare and endangered species.

In *The Haunted Canal*, which features in Young Puffin's Story Book series the author, Margaret Nash, combines all of these elements to produce a thrilling, ghostly adventure with a green theme. Her central characters, Jodie and Tom, have just built a raft. Not telling anyone, they launch the raft in the middle of the night and sail towards the tunnel where the ghost of Black Jack is said to have been seen:

They both sat with knees hunched and the raft swayed gently as the water slapped against it. A rising coolness wrapped around them, and the world was still. Jodie took a deep breath and the coldness went down her throat and made her cough.

'Shut up, you'll waken the dead,' said Tom.

Jodie shuddered. They drifted on a little way.

'Listen to the silence,' said Tom.

'Don't be daft, you can't hear silence,' said Jodie.

'You can.'

'Can't.'

'Can.' He dipped the piece of wood into the water and any silence there might have been was shattered with splashes, some of which landed on Jodie. She screwed her body up and groaned.

'Oh do it properly,' she said. 'Here, let me show you.' But Tom wouldn't be shown.

'I can do it,' he said, and bent over the side trying hard. Jodie watched her breath twirling out in front of her and dancing away with the moving mists.

The children go on to discover that the canal is polluted and the book describes in clear, easy to understand detail, how the Water Authority deals with the situation. Despite the inclusion of technical information, at no time does the author lose the thread of adventure and mystery which runs throughout the book, nor does she write down to her readership.

SCHOOL AND ANIMAL STORIES

Moving slightly up the age range, Anne Digby, author of the acclaimed Trebizon school stories, has produced a junior version in the form of Puffin's Jug Valley Junior series. In *The Headmaster's Ghost* she sets a ghostly tale against the background of school and the members of a good old secret club, a concept which is unmistakable to any former Famous Five or Secret Seven fan. Whilst the attitudes, social settings and dialogue of the characters have been skilfully and imaginatively updated, the appeal of the idea of belonging to a gang which solves mysteries guaranteed to baffle all adult understanding is, it would seem, as strong as it ever was.

Despite the fact that children adore animal stories, Dick King-Smith is one of the few contemporary authors concentrating on books featuring animals as their central characters. His award winning *The Sheep Pig* about a pig that believes it is a sheepdog, and more recent *Pretty Polly*, centred around Abigail and her pet hen Polly who she teaches to talk, are just two examples of his magically imaginative animal stories for younger readers.

Much material of this genre appears to place strong emphasis upon children or magical characters, rather than featuring anthropomorphised animals as the central character, telling the story from their own stylised viewpoint. Very often, animals play secondary roles to their child, wizard or witch counterpart within a contemporary book.

CHOOSE YOUR OWN ADVENTURE

Some years ago, the Choose Your Own Adventure series appeared in the bookshops. Within each book, the reader is asked to decide which action the central character should take. If he makes the wrong decision, the character comes to a sticky end but by making the right choice, the character will win through, escape, find the treasure or rescue the princess, and so on.

Initially, these books took the children's publishing world by storm but their popularity later diminished. An attempt to launch a similar series for the pre and primary school picture book market failed but in the higher age groups, they are still proving popular in the sci-fi and fantasy sections.

An examination of a choose your own adventure book will quickly reveal to the author that it is necessary, once having established your central character and background to the tale, to have several plots which will be contained within the one volume. Plotting the overall outline to the book takes on the nature of a multi-dimensional puzzle, for as the reader will, by his own choice, leap from one section of the book to another, the author must create each component part in such a way that it will interlock satisfactorily, without interrupting the flow of the story.

As an example, let us take as our central character, with whom the reader will identify, a knight of old, set against the background of King Arthur's court. Faced with the need to rescue a princess from the lair of a dragon, does he:

a) Charge at the dragon and kill it with his lance?
b) Find an ingenious way of putting out the dragon's fire?
c) Turn and run to live and fight another day?

Once the reader has made the choice, he will be instructed to

137

turn on to a specific page in the book. If he has chosen to kill the dragon, his subsequent choices may be:

a) To marry the princess.
b) To hold a dragon barbecue for the entire court to enjoy.
c) To take one look at the princess and to turn and run to live and woo another day.

The combination of choices are endless and provide the young reader with the opportunity to enjoy the book over and over again, arriving at one of a number of predictable endings by following a variety of books.

Once again, to appreciate fully the complexity of construction, should you wish to attempt a choose your own adventure book, the writer would be well advised to read as many books of this nature as possible.

Clearly, then, up to the age of eleven, the young reader enjoys a wide variety of material, designed to cater for the broad spectrum of humour, learning and adventure but life is soon to take on a more serious aspect, which will necessarily be accompanied by a far wider range of reading matter.

10
TEENS TO YOUNG ADULTS

It's all that the young can do for the old
is to shock them and keep them up to date.
George Bernard Shaw

The transition from junior to senior school can often be one of the most traumatic periods in a child's life. A change of school can bring with it the realisation that, in the new regime, they have become the last in life's pecking order. The sudden imposition of a new uniform, new disciplines, new studies and homework is combined with the physical and emotional demands of adolescence. Small wonder, then, that many parents will tell you that these were the most infuriating years of their child's growth.

Would-be writers for this age group must cast their minds back to their own early teens and truthfully acknowledge not only the agonies of indecision, lack of confidence, and outright rebellion that they experienced but must also acknowledge the impact their behaviour had upon those with whom they shared their lives.

It is, possibly, at around the age of eleven that the majority experience not only their change in attitudes but a definite shift in other people's attitudes toward themselves and the key word is 'responsibility'.

They must adapt themselves to the demands of a different environment, form new friendships and begin making decisions which will eventually have a profound effect on their future. Above all, the young teen will begin to ask 'Why?'. Not in the wide eyed innocently enquiring manner of the pre-school, for whom the world has yet to be discovered, but with the anxiety of a young adult, newly emerged from the chrysalis of childhood into an uncertain and possibly hostile environment in which their mood swings can be violent and unpredictable.

UNDERSTANDING THE ADOLESCENT

To understand fully the teen mind can be equated with attempting to find a plot in a plate of alphabet soup. The would-be writer for this age group will need to study their readers and their problems with a great deal of understanding and a loving heart. It is hard for the adult to cope with what, on one hand, may be skin-deep emotions and on the other, a genuine and often obsessive turmoil.

Not so long ago, perhaps only forty or fifty years, the years between eleven and the adult milestone of 21 were those in which the adolescent was disregarded as a potential market for specific targeting. In those years, the avid young reader would find their green junior library ticket withdrawn, to be replaced by a buff card giving them unrestricted entry to the adult shelves. Little or nothing existed to cater specifically for the intervening years, and many young readers leapt overnight from Arthur Ransome to Ian Flemming or from Enid Blyton to George Orwell.

Many readers from this generation were lost, unable to cope with the length and complexity of the adult novel, unable to accept the obscure adult priorities and unwilling to plough through page after page of lengthy description.

The deplorable gap has since been filled by authors who acknowledge the importance of the teenage child and its attendant problems. The writer for this age group has now a golden opportunity to take the emergent adolescent by the hand and, by cloaking the solution in a fictional setting, answer the many questions which beset the young mind, allay fears and generally educate.

THE CLASSIC TALE

However, there are a few exceptions to the rule which have

survived to become classics. *Treasure Island*, R.L. Stevenson's tale of the bravery of young Jim Hawkins in the face of Long John Silver and his wicked band of pirates, thrilled many a young heart with its promise of long lost treasure and the triumph of good over evil. Anna Sewell's *Black Beauty* captured the imagination of generations of horse lovers and her heart-stopping story of the beautiful black creature has survived as a much loved classic.

E. Nesbit's *The Railway Children*, in which two sisters and a young brother set out on a series of adventures, saving not only the lives of the passengers on a train but that of a foreign émigré and (with the help of an influential adult friend) bring about the release of their unjustly imprisoned father. The book not only features the first stirrings of romantic undertones between teenage boy and girl but clearly underlines the social and political influences of the day, while offering to the reader a compelling and thoroughly enjoyable story.

Perhaps one of the most notable classics still to be found on the bookshelves, written with an emphasis on the child's viewpoint, is Charles Kingsley's *The Water Babies*, where the grim reality of the suffering and degradation of the small children who were forced by their sweep masters into a terrifying network of chimneys was so graphically portrayed.

Many classics of this nature are, in fact, reprinted by publishing houses year after year and bought for today's children by schools and by the older generation, who remember them with affection.

Many of them, in the past, have formed part of the required reading list compiled by the educator, but emphasis in recent years has shifted. Whilst many would consider that the search for contemporary literature in the classroom has gone into overkill, with the inclusion of printed versions of some of the mindless television soap operas, the young mind can be well fed by today's authors, some of whom are already well on the way to becoming tomorrow's classics.

Just as the surviving classics dealt with the problems of the time in which they were written, so must the author for this age group encompass the problems which surround today's young teenage reader. They live in a high-tech world where computers are part of their everyday life, and would-be authors would do well to familiarise themselves with the relevant jargon should they wish to use a classroom of the 1990s as the setting for a story.

A giant among authors is undoubtedly Terry Pratchett, who has skilfully turned the world of fantasy fiction inside out for readers both young and old.

In his book *Only You Can Save Mankind* published by Doubleday, twelve year old computer games expert Johnny is unprepared for what happens when, in the opening stages of his new game, the Space Aliens surrender. As Terry Pratchett, through his young central character, points out, computer joysticks don't have a *Don't Fire* button.

Space warfare, peace treaties, starships, aliens and computer viruses all play a part in this thought provoking adventure, but it is an undeniable truth that there is nothing new under the sun. Many of Terry Pratchett's storylines may seem vaguely familiar to the adult reader, more than one of whom has seen the occasional similarity between the concept of his *Truckers* and Mary Norton's *Borrowers*.

It is the author's genius, however, in lifting the tale onto a new level of fantasy adventure, incorporating everything in the world of the contemporary reader, which has guaranteed his phenomenal success.

ESCAPISM OR REALISM?

The life of a contemporary child includes mountain bikes, Walkmans, skateboards, game-playing computers, designer clothes and access to pocket money well in excess of that doled out by parents of earlier generations. The failure to include at least a few of these in any contemporary story would immediately make it unbelievable to the reader.

Of far greater importance, however, are the newly acquired areas of interest and expression of emotional longing, coupled with the desire for unattainable achievements, such as becoming a pop-star, a champion athlete or winning the affection of the most desirable boy or girl in the school.

Parental caution is seldom accepted at its face value. The belief that the parent stands to gain something by insisting on a particular code of behaviour will often lead to stubborn resistance. Many teenagers, despite graphic warnings, are tempted in the search for new experiences to experiment with drink, drugs and sex. A recent survey funded by the Alcohol Education and Research Council discovered that a staggering 59 percent of schoolchildren in Manchester and Merseyside had been offered drugs and 36 percent claimed to have tried them; thirty percent admitted to drinking alcohol.

Conclusions drawn from the study were that over a third of children aged 14 and 15 have taken illegal drugs but in the main, hard drugs such as cocaine or heroin were widely rejected. It was felt that dabbling in drugs should be regarded as 'adolescent risk taking', feeding the need to feel they have become independent and assertive, when in fact they are unsure but are urged to test the parameters of their power by challenging authority with a show of bravado.

What they are trying to do is to establish their own identity, to escape the submissive yoke of childhood and to prove, whilst exhibiting often half-formed social skills, that they are 'grown up' and capable of making their own decisions.

To many a young teenager, the most important of the social skills is a sophisticated approach to the subject of sex. The need to discover its secrets, and uncover the mystique that surrounds what has become an undeniable urge, is paramount and the verbal foreplay, the whispering and giggling that are the first steps in life's mating dance can be seen taking place on any Saturday morning in any shopping precinct. It is not until these first approaches have been perfected that a pairing off takes place.

TEENAGE ROMANCE

The heartbreaking subject of young love is approached in books aimed at readers as young as eight years old. The Bantam series Sweet Valley Twins is aimed at the 8–11 year old age group. In *Big Brother's In Love* by Francine Pascal, Jessica and Elizabeth decide to help their older brother get over a broken romance. Whilst they themselves are not involved romantically, the young reader can learn a great deal about human relationships by looking in from the sidelines.

Focus on Love by Mary Anson is written for the 10+ age group in the Sweet Dreams series and tells the tale of Tiffany falling in love with the school's star athlete, Matt.

Yet another book in the same series, *Soap Star* by Francine Pascal, takes an in-depth look at today's teenage obsession with television soap operas. The author drives home the message that 'all that glitters is not gold', particularly in human relationships, when the central characters, overawed by the glamour of the star of the show, is foolish enough to drop the young boyfriend she really loves.

As the child matures, so does the depth of its feelings. The transition through the teen years and on into adult life is a constant process of learning to cope with the exhilaration of love and the heartache of loss or rejection.

Should you have decided by now to write for the teenage market, then not only must you create your characters but seriously consider the situations in which you intend to place them. The storyline needs, above all, to relate to some of the many problems which have a bearing on the life of the reader.

CURRENT TRENDS

The question of sexuality is not only one of interaction between boy and girl, in today's world it must also acknowledge the existence of feminism, lesbianism and homosexuality, any of which may be at the heart of the problem facing your central character.

Many books currently on sale deal with teenage pregnancy, abortion and, in some cases, social disease. Given a responsible treatment by the author, such books can often serve to answer the many questions that teenagers find difficult to voice aloud.

It is here that the first person viewpoint can provide the greatest impact. It is necessary to place the readers squarely in the shoes of the central character, enabling them to suffer or triumph or to undergo the many emotions endured by that character, many of which will already be within the range of their experience.

Girls in particular are concerned about their appearance or their weight and will identify with a character having this kind of problem. Many are in one-parent families as a result of divorce, bereavement or the failure of their parents to tie the marital knot. Despite today's tolerant views, almost every child would prefer to be part of a traditional two-parent family.

The illness of a mother or father, or indeed of the central character him or herself, can form the basis of a plot in a novel for this age group. Dealing with a situation such as this is not uncommon in real life and places an enormous emotional and physical burden upon the shoulders of the adolescent.

The darker side of teenage experience is yet another facet which, in recent years, has been sensitively explored by the caring author, as have child abduction and abuse.

Before condemning out of hand the use of drugs and alcohol, which often lead to vandalism and other crimes, the would-be author should consider the pressures to which the teenager is unwillingly subjected. The fear of failure, the long hours of study for examinations, the concern about the shortage of jobs once their schooldays are over; these cannot excuse their behaviour, but in some cases they can offer an explanation.

If sympathetically treated by the author, situations of this nature can, with reader identification, often point a way out of a downward behavioural spiral.

There are a few subjects, therefore, which would be considered taboo as a basis for a teenage novel. The author should set out to feed the imagination of the reader without pulling any punches.

It would be a disservice to the teenager to minimise difficulties or to bring about a simple contrived situation. However, by reading as much as you can for this particular age group, you will soon realise that not all is gloom and doom.

The subject of romance can be set against a strong mystery theme, where the central character is portrayed as a teenage sleuth or, more happily, liberally sprinkled with humour.

The supernatural or any sort of horror has a macabre fascination for this age group, and it is not necessary to pull any punches as many teenagers will already have delved into the works of Stephen King, Graham Masterson and the like.

FANTASY FICTION

The world of science fiction has changed dramatically from the tales of early space explorers. Space has now been conquered and the writer must look to a new sort of adventure.

Terry Pratchett's *Discworld* is a fine example of this particular genre. Eric, the title character in *Discworld* (published by Gollancz) and inhabitant of this magical world, is a demonology hacker through whom the author deals with many taboo subjects in an irreverent and hilarious romp.

Dealt with in this manner, science fiction remains in the mind of the average reader as pure fantasy. However, genuine concern has been expressed in recent years following a report that a tiny percentage of young readers became so obsessed with the books in the mould of *Dungeons & Dragons* (the role playing fantasy adventure game) that they lose their hold on reality and can sometimes be unable to differentiate between the game and real life.

1992 saw the tenth anniversary of *Fighting Fantasy* books and the publication by Puffin of a volume to commemorate the anniversary, gathering together in its yearbook mean monsters, vile beasts and cruel conquerors in a land of legend, where epic battles and heroic deeds take place. If you feel that this is a genre to which you can contribute, then this must be on your list of essential reading.

ANIMALS, CONSERVATION AND SPORTING STORIES

From fantasy to fact and into the realms of animal life which is, and always has been, threatened by man. On the one hand there are many books with strong green themes, making teenage readers aware of the harm being done globally to flora and fauna alike.

There are also a handful of beautifully written books which use a living animal as their central character. In *Watership Down* the whole story is sensitively told through the eyes of animals. The reader, having identified with the gentle rabbit, suffers his agonies and triumphs and learns to appreciate how the world of today affects wildlife in general.

Irish author Tom McCaugren has to his credit a trilogy of remarkable wildlife books, the first of which *Run With The Wind* won the Children's Book Award of the Reading Association of Ireland; another *Run Swift Run Free*, was the winner of the Medal for Young People's Books in the Irish book awards.

In the story of young foxes who face the dangers of modern living, the characters are forced to learn how to fend for themselves. The anthropomorphised animals exist in a hostile world and the author offers to the reader the opportunity to draw a parallel between the problems surrounding the growing fox and those surrounding the growing teenager.

When catering for the many areas of teenage development, it is necessary to include the world of sport. Despite the media passion for downgrading the average youngster, portraying them as idle, unfit, unwashed and undernourished, the truth is that a high proportion are fanatically obsessed with one of a variety of sports and athletic skills. The young reader who aspires to success in such areas will search the shelves for titles which exhibit the knowledge for which he or she thirsts, coupled with a story of success.

RACISM AND MINORITY GROUPS

Racism and the problems faced by ethnic minorities are increasingly being tackled by contemporary authors. But before embarking on what is by definition a highly sensitive area, be sure of your ground. Personal experience and in-depth knowledge are essential if the writer is to avoid patronising or offending the very readership at which the book is aimed.

147

BBC chiefs recently took the decision to reject plans for a series based on the schoolboy character from *Greyfriars*, Billy Bunter. They felt it would encourage children to overeat and get fat.

Similarly, publishers Hodder & Stoughton, having modernised and sanitised Enid Blyton's Noddy, removing all mention of Golliwogs, renaming Miss Slap the schoolmistress, and censoring all references to Noddy and Big Ears sharing a bed, turned their attention to the Famous Five books.

Expressions such as *he looks a bit queer* and *let the girls get the picnic stuff ready* have been suitably updated to avoid any impression of homosexuality or feminism. References to class differences, racial and regional stereotyping have also been removed or rewritten in such a way that is thought to be more acceptable in today's multi-racial society.

Whether these alterations have improved the books or, as some purists would assert, have ruined the flavour and feel of the stories, is a matter of personal opinion. Only time will tell how well these new versions fare against the tried, tested and much loved original publications.

HISTORICAL SETTINGS

Despite the current trend towards contemporary settings, historical and time-slip novels, providing escapist adventure combined with detailed information about the era in which they are set, are still much in demand by the teenage reader.

In his novel *The Tiger In The Well* (published by Puffin) Philip Pullman managed to combine a graphic picture of the political and social life of Victorian Europe with the story of a young independent woman's fight against evil. The central character was a single mother, who runs her own business and is a feminist, yet the setting is Victorian London.

Current trends in the historical novel suggest a marked interest in the second world war and the consequences of the Holocaust. Stories documenting life in Germany in the months before the war, the attitudes in this country as the news of what was going on filtered through, the influx of foreign refugees, and British evacuees are finding favour with publishers and young readers alike.

Humour for this age group is quirky and unrestrained. Satirical, wry humour, usually against the Establishment and commenting upon the unfairness of life supersedes the slapstick style preferred in books for younger children. Once again, Terry Pratchett immediately springs to mind as being synonymous with the quirky irreverent style that teenagers enjoy.

Having then reviewed the market and acknowledged the wide range of subject matter which forms the basis of today's teenage fiction, let us begin to look at the marketplace in which you will sell your work. Magazines will be our starting point, and once again the key is market research.

The current edition of *The Writer's & Artist's Yearbook* will provide a list of comics and magazines suitable for the teenage reader. It may, however, be necessary for you to double check with your newsagent whether the publication is still alive and well as, over the years, magazines have been seen to rise and fall in a dramatically short space of time.

W.H. Smith publish a very useful free publication quarterly, listing every magazine and comic for children, teenagers and adults available at the time. If you ask the manager at your local branch, he will tell you when the next one is due. These publications are keenly sought after and you would be well advised to act promptly if you wish to obtain a copy.

Having targeted a group of magazines for which you feel you may well be able to provide material, the next step is to purchase copies over a period of several weeks and to familiarise yourself thoroughly with the content, sending for editorial guidelines from those with which you feel you have a particular empathy.

Having familiarised yourself with the market in general, and perhaps selected one or two target magazines, the next step will of course be the all-important idea. Whilst reading many of the published stories, you may well have thought to yourself, 'I would have written a different ending to that' or 'With a different background or problem, the tale would have taken on a completely different twist'. Many new ideas for teenage fiction are born in the mind of the author in this

149

manner, but turn to the problem page in the same magazine and you will find the letters to the editor (and the accompanying replies) provide wonderful material from which to cut your own storyline. They will outline the many areas of concern which are paramount in the mind of the young reader.

Once again, allow yourself to eavesdrop, unnoticed of course, on telephone conversations, public transport, works' canteens, in fact any venue where young people gather together to discuss their problems.

An author of my acquaintance often finds inspiration from some of today's song lyrics and, as long as you can actually understand the words that are being sung, you will find that many of them reflect the world as seen through teenage eyes.

We have already examined the many picture-strip stories you will find in comics and magazines, but now is the time to turn your attention to those which appear in text.

Generally speaking, the format for teenage stories falls into one of three distinct categories. The first and often shortest are centred around the emotional personal experience of your central character and are often written in the first person.

The second are of greater length and greater complexity. Careful plotting and a variety of characters can be skilfully brought into play to bring the story to a point of crisis which will then be solved in a satisfactory manner.

A careful analysis of work already published will quickly reveal such essential factors as the editorial preference with regard to length, content, number of characters and so forth. A written analysis will also reveal whether the story is written in the first or third person, whether the magazine favours a sad or a happy ending and whether the editor is prepared to accept flashbacks within the storyline.

Pay a great deal of attention to the way in which the author of the story has strengthened or weakened his central character by carefully sketching in the social background, desires and achievements, together with the involvement of the other characters within the story.

Pay particular attention to the construction of the story.

Ideally, the point of entry should be at the moment of change in the main character's life. Short opening sentences and paragraphs will more readily grab the attention of the reader, particularly if they are sprinkled with plenty of action or dialogue.

CONFLICT AND PACE

In a published story, you will probably find the central character will be introduced as quickly as possible, together with at least a suggestion of the conflict to come. The secret is to dive straight into the story and keep the pace moving throughout.

Language should be simple and descriptions should be short. If longer descriptive passages are necessary to the storyline, then break them up with dialogue which should be constantly used to flesh your characters and move the story forward.

If your central character resolves the major problem too quickly, then your story is finished. It is far better to swing the character towards and then away from the final solution by placing new obstacles in the path and so prolonging the interest and involvement of the reader.

The third, and highly popular, category for this age group is the confession story. Although it is clearly fiction, it is nonetheless written in such a manner that it appears to be real life. The formula of sin, suffer and repent used in the adult confession story is somewhat softened, but is still used to outline the fact that the central character has transgressed in some way. This will have placed her in the sad and sorry state of learning from her errors, and the story finally offers advice to readers who may find themselves in similar circumstances.

Written in the first person, these stories must be convincing. The teenage central characters must find themselves in what undoubtedly appear to be genuine situations. They are designed to be helpful and satisfying, in that the central character will have learned and gained emotional stature from her experience. The style needs to reflect the manner in which teenagers confide in one another, but on no account should the author blatantly attempt to moralise.

Once the story is written, go back and read it, preferably aloud. Ask yourself: Does it ring true? Is the dialogue authentic? Have you made the most of the emotional factor? How do you feel about the central character (the one with whom, you hope, your reader will establish a relationship)? Have you maintained the supremacy of your character through the story, or has a minor character taken over that all-important role?

The ending does not always have to be happy, but if it has a note of sadness then it must be upbeat, offering to the reader that distant light on the horizon.

Once the idea is born, it will quickly become obvious whether the tale you wish to tell can be told in the space of a short story or whether, due to its complexity or timespan, it will need the space provided within the pages of a teenage novel. All that has gone before in the way of understanding your reader and market research is relevant to a work of novel length.

The main difference lies in the constituents of the tale. A short story will, of necessity, occupy only a short period in time, perhaps a few days. The number of characters will be limited to avoid confusion, and in all probability the author will deal with only a single problem.

When planning a novel, however, the timespan may encompass several weeks or even a few months. There is the writing space to create several changes of scene and to incorporate many more characters and problems. However, throughout the 30,000 or 50,000 word required length, the story should be well planned to move rapidly from the beginning to a satisfying and inevitable conclusion.

In David Williams' *Forgive and Forget* (published by Pan Books Heartlines series) his central character, Claire, has her life thrown into turmoil when her family is forced to move to Wales. She leaves behind Simon, the boy who means so much to her, in a mood of determination that under no circumstances will she come to like her new home. Eventually, however, new friends and the rugged beauty of the countryside soothe away her resentment. Inevitably, a new boy comes onto the scene and Gareth, the dark eyed Welsh boy, captures her with his infectious grin, making her forget all about Simon.

Written in the first person, the story plunges immediately into an emotional high point in Claire's day, on the first page of Chapter One:

> I walked out of the main entrance to the Priory Grange Comprehensive School, clutching the small computerised result slip in my hand. Though it was only ten-thirty, the August sun was warm, heralding another sizzling summer day. I shook my head with incredulity and glanced again at the strip of paper to make sure I'd read it correctly. There, printed in small regular letters, were my 'O' level results. I felt elation bubble up inside me, washing away my disbelief, and making me feel light-headed.
>
> Then someone called my name, and turning, I saw Simon Fenton running across the yard. I'd been so excited that I'd forgotten to wait for him while he went to collect his own results.
>
> Just over six feet tall, with fair wavy hair that flopped untidily over a broad tanned forehead, he was one of the best-looking guys in the fifth form.

Claire's elation, however, is shortlived when she is presented with the fait accompli of the family's removal from all that is familiar to what she sees as a friendless future.

Grudgingly, over a period of time, she comes to accept the inevitable and, upon moving into her new home, finds Gareth fishing from the river which runs through the garden. Immediately, there is a conflict similar to that found in the works of many writers for the bestselling series of romantic novels by Mills & Boon. Skilfully, through the eyes of his central character, the author with a mix of dialogue and action, totally involves the reader in Claire's predicament:

> He spun round at the sound of my angry voice and gaped as though he'd never seen a girl in his life. Then,

recovering, he hurried towards me.

'Hey, I'm sorry... I didn't see you standing behind me.' The soft Welsh lilt to his voice sounded like music in my ears. But it wasn't that which made me catch my breath – or the fact that he was taller than I'd first assumed. It was his eyes. They were dark brown with a depth and clarity that made me feel weak. And he had the longest eyelashes I'd ever seen on a guy.

'Hold on!' Deftly, he threaded the hook through my sweater and, taking a knife from his pocket, cut through the line. 'I don't think I've done any damage.'

He looked down at me, and the smile that came so naturally to his lips melted the anxious concern in his eyes, and once more I found myself catching my breath. Then he went and spoilt it.

'But what were you doing there anyway?' he said. 'It was a stupid thing to do. You should have known better than to stand right behind someone who was casting.'

'Oh was it?' His bluntness annoyed me and I began to think that first impressions could certainly be deceptive.

'Of course it was. The hook could have sunk right into you.'

The concern was there in those dark eyes again and once more I felt butterflies fluttering deep inside my stomach.

'You haven't answered me. What were you doing there?'

'I might well ask you the same question,' I said stiffly.

He shrugged his broad shoulders, 'I was fishing, wasn't I?'

'That was obvious. But you happen to be fishing from my garden.'

To quote any further passages or indeed, to tell you how the story ends would be to cheat you out of the pleasure of reading the book for yourself, something recommended to anyone considering writing for this age group.

Once you have, in your mind, firmly established your

characters and the outline for your book, then write your synopsis, spreading it over ten or twelve chapters.

Many authors use a storyboard, a large chart ruled into the relevant number of squares, each representative of a chapter. Into each square, they note in pencil the relevant place in time and the entry and exit of each character, the background, the forward movement in the story and the necessary points of conflict between the characters.

The pencilled chart can be altered at will until the whole story can be pictured as a satisfying series of scenes. Once the serious work of writing begins, a chart of this nature can provide an invaluable blueprint to follow.

Submission of the manuscript to a publisher can be either in the form of the completed book, or the first three chapters with a synopsis of the rest of the story. A simple covering letter containing a brief personal introduction to the publisher and voicing the hope that he will find it suitable for publication is sufficient. Always remember to include return postage and be prepared to wait, sometimes for as long as three months, for him to reveal his decision.

Remember that once your story is told and you have despatched the manuscript, it is more than possible you will feel intense loneliness. The characters with whom you have lived for so long will seemingly have deserted you and there is only one answer: start another book without delay. Whilst the first is making its way around the publishing world, you should be well on the road to producing a second or even a third novel for teenagers.

11
OTHER
MARKETS

*The most imaginative people are the most credulous
for to them everything is possible.*
Alexander Chase

There is within us all a little of the exhibitionist, a desire to
express ourselves, to enjoy the approval of an audience and
often that desire begins in childhood.

WRITING FOR THE STAGE

It is not hard to think back to one's schooldays and
remember the excitement of watching, or better still taking
part in, the Nativity or end of term play.

An innovative teacher can bring a dull period to life by
directing her class to enact scenes from history or literature,
for the fun of role playing will ensure that the lesson is better
remembered than if it is simply read out loud from the text-
book page.

Many enthusiastic teachers write their own scripts for the
children in their care. Knowing the strengths and weaknesses
of their cast, the length of time to be allowed on the
programme and the limitations of costume and set, they are
indeed in an advantageous position. Yet again, from the
writer's point of view, the importance of involvement cannot
be stressed too strongly.

Few schools are without a Parent Teachers Association of
some sort and it is often from the seedbed of their meetings
and discussions that new ideas spring into being. If you feel
you can contribute your writing skills to a future drama

production, then take the opportunity to offer your services.

The first thing you will need will be, as always, an idea. In a script for the very young primary schoolchild, you may favour the reworking of a nursery rhyme or fairy tale. You may, however, have something original in mind, perhaps with a green theme, incorporating a cast of animals or a folk tale from a faraway land.

MEET YOUR ACTORS AND CHECK THE VENUE

Within the realms of reason, costumes and sets for the under eleven schoolchild present few problems to teachers and willing parents. Whilst the play itself will be carried by the strength of the main characters, woe betide the playwright who does not allow each child a chance to shine, albeit with only a single line of dialogue. The words the actors are required to speak should be simple to say and to the point, the sentences short and easy to memorise.

It is, of course, a plus factor if you have some experience of theatre, whether it has been gained on the amateur or professional stage. If this experience is lacking, then the would-be playwright should try to join a local drama group, not necessarily to take a speaking part in a production but to become involved in some way.

Local groups of players will readily welcome that extra pair of hands to shift scenes or to assist with lighting or wardrobe. An invaluable sense of theatre can be gained from backstage and once established as a welcome member of the group, you may well find the opportunity to produce an original script for performance in front of an audience.

We have already looked closely at the technique involved in picture-strip writing and if you feel that you have an affinity with this then you will find it is a short step to producing a manuscript suitable for the stage; there are many similarities in the technique.

As always, your first requirement will be the storyline, which may be contemporary, fantasy or historical. Next, your main characters need to be thoroughly explored and woven into the background of your tale. The set against which your play will unfold will be governed by certain limitations. An end of term play for the under elevens will, undoubtedly, be presented in the main hall of the school, many of which have their own movable staging and overhead rail upon which curtains are hung for the occasion. Many schools are, however, without such refinements and you will need to adapt your script accordingly, and additional scenery and props should be kept to a minimum to avoid over-complication.

SCRIPT LAYOUT

The layout of your manuscript should begin with the scene setting:

Scene: A woodland glade. A rabbit is fast asleep at the foot of a tree. A squirrel enters stage right.

Squirrel: (Looking worried, sees rabbit. Crosses stage and prods rabbit awake) Wake up, wake up, they're coming.

Rabbit: (Wakes, rubs eyes, stretches and yawns) What's that you say? Who's coming?

Squirrel: The owl and the weasel and the dormouse too.

Rabbit: (Puzzled) Coming here? But why?

Squirrel: (Impatiently) We're having a meeting to decide what to do. Don't you remember? I told you.

Rabbit: Oh yes, I remember now. The wood is in danger.

Squirrel: That's right. The humans are going to cut down all the trees.

Rabbit: (Crossly, flexing his muscles) Not if we can stop them (Points into wings) Look, here come the others now.

Once you have written your play to the required length, which you will have ascertained during discussions with the teaching staff, read it aloud before submitting it, and if possible attend the first rehearsal to correct any faults or omissions in your dialogue by rewriting on the spot. If possible, incorporate music into your play for the younger age group, keeping the lyrics simple and the tune familiar.

Older children of eleven plus are far more ambitious and a writer of my acquaintance made a name for herself by adapting several classics for performance by this age group. Working with the school's music master and an eager cast of young thespians, her version of *Cyrano de Bergerac* was recently presented as a full-length musical, receiving rave reviews and assuring her of an annual demand for more of the same.

Once your play has been written and performed, it is then possible to offer it for publication to one of several markets: Century Hutchison, Chatto & Windus, and Pan Books all publish drama scripts.

RADIO AND TELEVISION OPPORTUNITIES

Should you wish to turn your talents to writing for radio, then you will find the same freedom which exists within the technique of picture-strip writing when creating a tale destined to be drawn frame by frame by an artist, rather than captured on film by a photographer. The use of sound has the same limitless borders within which the author may work, employing a combination of sound effects, dialogue and music.

It is possible to create in the mind of the listener the picture of a gypsy encampment, an eastern bazaar or a school playing field, or indeed to incorporate all three into one story, changing the set at will.

The market for children's radio drama has narrowed considerably from the halcyon days of children's hour, when young listeners were eager to tune in between five and six o'clock for an hour's programming devoted entirely to their needs.

You may remember the wonderful dramatisations of *Wind In The Willows* and *The House At Pooh Corner* and the voices of Larry The Lamb and Dennis The Daschund who brought to life *The Tales Of Toytown*.

Opportunities do exist, but now mainly in the area of BBC schools broadcasting. A full explanation of how you should approach the market can be found in the handbook *Writing For The BBC* which can be bought from the BBC Shop, 35 Marylebone High Street, London W1M 4AA and you can obtain details of their annual programme schedule from BBC Educational Broadcasting Services, Villiers House, Ealing Broadway, London W5 2PA.

When, in 1990, the BBC launched Radio 5, there is no doubt that they had every intention of including a good variety of children's drama. In a letter dated 16th October 1990, replying to an initial query regarding children's programmes, Caroline Raphael, Editor, Children & Youth, Drama and Features, Radio Five, made the following statement:

Please note that we are not in a position to commission material on the basis of a synopsis or proposal only from writers whose work we do not know or have not previously broadcast.

She did, however, go on to outline Radio 5's planned schedule in which she intended to offer, from Mondays to Fridays, a fifteen minute reading slot aimed at seven to eleven year olds. In addition to these readings, she intended to feature, on Mondays, both original and dramatised material for ten to thirteen year olds, exploring emotional issues and 'a full range of other genres'. Tuesdays and Wednesdays were to feature 25 minutes of original and dramatised material; Thursdays were to offer a thirty minute dramatisation of a classic tale; and twice a week Radio 5 was to offer a thirty minute late night drama slot for ages fourteen upwards, which was to include original drama as well as dramatisation of popular young adult fiction.

Two years on, towards the end of 1992, Radio 5's schedule sadly bears little relation to those hopeful beginnings. Mondays and Wednesdays offer a 45 minute drama serial by Hunter Davis set in the sixth form of a comprehensive school and fifteen minute readings from a novel by Anne Fine for seven to ten year olds. Apart from the daily readings from Ann Fine's novel, there is no other fiction for children, drama or otherwise, except a Sunday programme featuring dramatisations of Tolkein's Hobbit tales.

160

Whilst Radio 5 does its best to feature programmes specifically for a younger audience, it is beginning to look as though BBC Radio is gradually giving up the fight to compete with its great rival, television.

Many authors, however, dream of seeing their work on the small screen and some achieve that pinnacle of desire. It is not, however, an easy market to break into. The majority of writers for television are professionals who have perfected the necessary techniques and have become established within the minds of the programme planners as reliable writers, instinctively aware of the need to work within a budget. A limited number of sets, characters and special effects are second nature to the experienced television playwright.

If, nonetheless, you are determined to see your name roll with the credits, then you should watch everything that is currently offered to the young viewer. This could, however, be a very depressing exercise as even on the BBC, whose reputation in this area is high, air time for children is devoted, in the main, to a non-stop diet of imported cartoons.

BBC School Television, in common with BBC Radio, offers one of the few openings for freelance writers. According to Jacqueline Johnston (Chief Assistant, School Broadcasting) they do employ freelance writers but only 'on an ad hoc basis'. She advises anyone wishing to pursue the possibilities to contact Judy Whitfield (Executive Producer of primary series) at BBC School Television, White City, 201 Wood Lane, London W12 7TS (Tel: 081-752 5252).

With the growth of satellite television, which has to fill large amounts of air time, independent production companies are concentrating on inexpensive animated series which they can sell to television stations on a global basis.

The new ITV stations will be required by Government legislation to provide at least ten hours' of children's broadcasting per week, covering all ages and areas of entertainment, drama and information. Whilst the Independent Television Commission has a brief to monitor these programmes for violence and language, quality is hardly mentioned.

Yet again, we return to market assessment and appreciation, despite the apparent lack of opportunity; even established writers had to start somewhere. If, therefore, you discover what you consider to be an opening equal to your talent, then contact the individual producer of the programme or independent production company with an outline of your idea. It may just hold the attention of the programme planner and you will find yourself with your foot on the first rung of the ladder to success.

THE WORLD OF NEWSPAPERS

As a complete change of pace, the aspiring writer for children should not overlook the world of newspapers. Setting aside the obvious specialist columns written for the adult reader, there often remains the opportunity for a children's page which, once established, can provide an enjoyable outlet for both the reader and the writer.

Begin by researching local and regional newspapers within a twenty mile radius of your home. If you come across a publication that already sets aside editorial space for a variety of regular columns, the editor may well consider an additional column for children. If, however, little local editorial is featured, the editor might be willing to consider its inclusion as a way of bolstering interest in his newspaper.

Editorial addresses of local and regional newspapers are listed in *Willings Press Guide*, a copy of which may be found at your local library. Once you have researched your market, send a letter of enquiry, a brief CV containing relevant details of your writing experience and outline of the proposed content of your page, together with return postage.

Among the 'thank you, but no thank you' responses, may well be either a letter or a phone call from an interested editor. It is imperative, at this point, that you convince him not only of your ability to write the page to the required length but also of your reliability in unfailingly delivering your copy in pristine condition to meet his required deadlines.

A children's column can occupy a space on the page from as little as a quarter tabloid to a full broadsheet and may be as brief as a chatty, informative letter to the reader or a mix of features, local news, competitions, birthday club and fillers.

The subject matter for features will be governed partly by age, but will generally cover a wide spectrum of interest: sports, hobbies, holidays, green issues, local history, conservation and local events, anniversary items and children who have achieved or are involved in something worthy of note.

With regard to local events and conservation issues, an enquiry to the amenities department of your local town hall will provide you with a list of relevant organisations. Contact their secretaries and ask to be put on their mailing lists, or to be invited along to meetings, so that you may become involved with the aims of the organisation.

The same department at your local town hall will be able to furnish you with a schedule of future events to take place throughout the area. Should they be of interest to your young readers, then you will be in a position to give them advance publicity. Bear in mind, however, that the editor will require your copy to be provided well in advance of publication dates. Unlike hard news, which has a fleeting 'shelf-life', editorial space is set aside for regular features and contributors must plan well ahead to ensure their column carries material relevant to seasonal dates and local events.

Over the past few years, holidays designed exclusively for children unaccompanied by adults have been extremely popular. They offer a wide variety of activities for children of all ages. A visit to your travel agent will provide you with a list of the tour operators' names, addresses and brochures. Once again, write and ask to be put on their mailing lists. A well informed feature on this subject should be welcomed by an editor.

Every town has its young sporting enthusiasts and it is possible to encourage the readers themselves to supply copy for publication in the form of a report on a recent notable triumph. Today's child has access to a wide range of hobbies and activities and it is in this field that you may well find children suitable for interview, due to their achievements.

A regular column on the junior page could well be devoted

to a feature of this nature and you will find yourself inundated with youngsters keen to shine in print if you begin by publishing a request for readers to write in with the relevant information.

Should you receive a letter from the child itself, then check with the parent that they are aware that you have been invited to their home to interview their offspring. Make a convenient appointment and turn up on time. Children are quick to detect a sham, so your interest must be genuine and your enthusiasm for the subject matter of your interview be convincing.

Having armed yourself with a list of questions to which you will require answers, put the child at ease and then let him or her talk. Make your notes and ask questions where necessary, but informality is a most important factor when interviewing a child. Take your own camera along to capture that all important photograph, or ask your editor whether he will arrange an independent photocall with the newspaper's official photographer.

Many professional journalists will throw up their hands in horror at the final piece of advice and that is to check your copy with the child or parent before submitting it for publication. In this instance, you are not a national journalist looking for hard news or digging for dirt. By checking your copy, even over the telephone, you will ensure that you have the facts right and that when the child appears in school on the day of publication, it will not be subjected to ridicule by its peers, thereby turning what should have been a proud and enjoyable moment into a period of abject misery.

Once you have made a friend of the interviewee, you will often find that they become the source of information which, in turn, will produce an ongoing supply of interesting copy. Once again, however, as mentioned in Chapter Three, a word of caution: the writer should never forget that children are vulnerable, and your innocent publication of that photograph and article featuring an attractive child could well lead to the unwelcome attention from some of today's wierdos. Never publish the child's full address or telephone number. The name and the town are quite sufficient. Should anyone wish to make contact due to mutual interest, then all communications should be diverted through you on the understanding that you will pass them on, preferably to the parent.

BOOK REVIEWS, JOKES AND COMPETITIONS

Fillers can be of any length and cover any subject but would usually fall into the category of an Ask Me Another column, where you might invite questions from children which you, the columnist, will answer. You may have your own set of encyclopedia or other reference books. If not, a trip to your library and a little research will soon provide the answers.

Invite your readers to send in jokes to fill a *Giggles & Groans* column, making sure you publish the name of each contributor.

A book review column can be beneficial in many ways. Begin by inviting would-be reviewers of all ages to write to you, setting out their age, interests and reading preferences. Contact some of the major publishing houses, explain your intention to them and ask them to send you review copies at regular intervals.

Provide each reader with a book suitable for their age group and within their range of interest. Write to them enclosing a list of the comments they need to include in their review and give them a deadline, allowing them to keep the book as your thank you for their efforts.

Many reviews will be returned quickly, with a request for another book. If no review is forthcoming, then the child's name should be removed from your panel of reviewers. You will undoubtedly have to sub-edit some of their work but it is essential that you publish their viewpoint, warts and all. It is a golden opportunity for the child's own voice to be heard and you will find that it is a very popular part of your page. An added bonus for the writer is that, by receiving advance copies of current publications, it enables you to keep your finger on the pulse of what both the child and publisher finds currently pleasing.

Riddles and word puzzles also make excellent copy but if you really wish to catch a potential editor's eye and to provide a regular page in a newspaper, then the most important factor on a junior page is a weekly competition which offers a prize.

PRIZES AND ADMINISTRATION

Prizes can be obtained from a variety of sources. To begin with, some publishing houses, once you are on their mailing list, will regularly offer a quantity of books in a specific series or by a specific author as the basis for a competition. A local bookshop eager for publicity may well be coerced into offering a few volumes for the same reason.

Toy shops in the area may often be prepared to supply a few small items, again in return for free publicity, but the best source of supply is the toy manufacturers themselves. A trip to a national toy fair, Earls Court and Harrogate are the largest, will open your eyes to the astonishing variety of new toys destined to become the sought-after playthings throughout the coming year.

Try to avoid the official press day, and go well prepared. Have with you a supply of sample published pages, a copy of the newspaper, details of its circulation figures and the area it serves and a list of the deadlines for which you require competition prizes.

Some companies have a public relations department within their organisation; others use an outside public relations company to handle publicity matters. Whatever the case, ask to speak to someone who will be in a position to agree to provide you with the requisite number of prizes, but beware: many rash promises are made that are not always honoured. You should, therefore, immediately upon your return home, write to confirm dates and prize values with the company concerned and ask for their acknowledgement and confirmation before building the competition into your schedule. Some will be eager to help and others reluctant, but you will soon find those that you can trust and work with happily over a long period of time.

Some companies will provide you with a package deal, devising their own competitions and providing you with comprehensive copy containing such essential elements as an accurate description of the item, their trademark or logo and a black/white photograph or colour slide of the prize to be won. Others will simply agree to your offering a specific toy as a competition prize and willingly leave you to do the rest, providing you with as little as a photograph, brief description and retail price of the item. In this case, you will need to write your own copy and devise a simple word grid or a series of words relevant to the prize, in which you have jumbled the letters for the child to sort into an intelligible answer.

Your young readers, sad to say, will not happily involve themselves in an competition which requires a list of questions to be answered or contains a tie-breaker. Should you decide to try this sort of competition, you will notice a distinct drop in the size of your competition entry, as will your editor.

To devise a colouring competition, unless you are a gifted artist and can produce your own drawings, can prove prohibitively expensive. Many companies can provide you with suitable artwork, which can be used in one of two ways, either as a colour competition (in which case you will find an enthusiastic response to the competition and judging may well take several hours of your time), or as a spot the difference competition. The latter format simply involves photocopying the artwork and blanking out ten minor details on one copy. Readers are then asked to 'spot the differences' between the two published pictures and prizes are awarded to the first correct entries drawn out of the postbag. Incidentally, the entry for a colouring competition should, of course, bear the child's age as each entry must be judged on an age and ability basis.

In fact, entry forms for all children's competitions must request their age as more often than not, if the rules fail to stipulate that the entrants must be under sixteen, you will find a large number of hopeful adults entering your competitions.

Having judged the competition, you should then notify the winners by post, either enclosing the prize if you have selected to deal with this part of the administration yourself, or telling them that they should allow 28 days for delivery of the item should it be coming direct from the manufacturers. It is then necessary to send a tear sheet of the page, featuring the relevant competition, to the manufacturer or public relations contact, together with the names and addresses of the winners and, if they are not in your possession, your request that the prizes be despatched direct to the children immediately.

Should there be an unavoidable delay, ask your contact to write to the winners and explain the circumstances. Once again, you will soon sort out who you can rely on and who should be removed from the competition list.

Bear in mind when selling the idea of a competition as part of your junior page to a prospective editor that, when you negotiate a fee, you take into account the expenses involved. Setting up competitions can run into considerable expenditure, your visits to toy fairs, telephone calls, postage and time spent in administration can, very quickly, wipe out any profit you may make.

Having once made contact with a variety of manufacturers and public relations companies, they will regularly supply you with product information and should you find yourself short of copy, they will welcome the appearance on your page of a straightforward product shot and a little information concerning availability and price.

Once again, the effort involved in being included on the mailing list of any company which produces any commodity for the young reader will prove to be invaluable, particularly if your page is destined to be read specifically by teenagers. In this event, the mix of copy will alter slightly.

It may be that the editorial requirement is for a percentage of your page to be aimed at the teenage reader or you may have been commissioned to produce a column entirely catering for that age group. In either case, you will need to consider new areas of interest reflecting those of the reader.

Once again, bear in mind the obsessions which colour the life of the 11+ child. Fashion, cosmetics, dating, pop music, videos and films will be areas of interest which must influence your copy. Should a page for this age group include personal dialogue with the reader, often seen in the form of a personal experience feature or a reply to a reader's letter, then great care should be taken by the writer to appear ageless. No matter what your adult viewpoint on a subject may be, always bear in mind the age and attitudes of your reader. Dare to talk down or to patronise and your following will disappear overnight. It is a difficult line to tread but experience, and hopefully feedback from your readers, will place your feet more confidently on the path as time goes by.

Whilst on the subject of newspapers there has, in recent years, been a growing interest in the production of newspapers specifically designed for children. Possibly the market leader in this category is *Early Times* which has grown from a small acorn into a large, well informed and well read oak, underlining the young reader's desire to be both entertained and educated.

Many major industries produce literature, most of which is directed at the schoolchild, which graphically explains the workings of such things as a coal mine, a gas station, an electricity generating plant or a nuclear complex.

The magazine world, conscious of the thirst for knowledge, have produced Partworks, series of magazines covering many aspects of today's hi-tech world. Series exploring history, the world of medicine, and general knowledge have all been collected eagerly for future reference by young enthusiasts.

You should, by now, appreciate the remarkable scope available to the writer for children. Whatever your own idea of knowledge and expertise, whatever your personal choice with regard to fiction, everything in your adult experience can be put to use when writing for the younger reader.

12
AGENTS, SYNDICATION AND RECORD KEEPING

Great editors do not discover nor produce great authors.
Great authors produce great publishers.

John Farrar

Whilst the publishing industry as a whole has had its problems, it appears that the sales of children's books are as buoyant as ever. Undoubtedly the market is competitive, but parents do continue to buy books for their children. Today's publisher, in a bid for maximum sales, produces publicity in the form of exciting promotions and display material, in outlets which have expanded far beyond the traditional bookshop.

The quality of books have improved as a result of value for money buying by parents, teachers, librarians and of course, the booksellers themselves. Therefore, before a publisher will consider accepting your manuscript, he must be sure in his own mind that your books will sell, not only to British markets but, when taken to one of the many international book fairs, to overseas markets as well.

This is where an agent can be worth his weight in gold, and ten percent of your earnings can be a small price to pay for one who is efficient. Finding an agent, however, is perhaps one of the most difficult tasks faced by an author, so before deciding whether you actually need one, let us first establish exactly what they do.

WHAT DOES AN AGENT DO?

To begin with, the agent's income is derived from the income of the authors he or she represents. It is, therefore, clearly within their interests to promote each author's work in order to sell it as widely, and for the highest price, as possible. It is from these sales that agents deduct their fee and it is, therefore in their best interests to find the best deal for their authors, which may in some cases include the negotiation and sale of subsidiary rights such as broadcasting, television and film.

Their specialist skills lie in the fact that they have a keen sense when reading a manuscript of what will or will not conform to the current market requirements. Through their unique relationship with the publishing world, they know instinctively at which editor the work should be directed. Their finger on the pulse of the market will be far more sensitive than that of the writer, due to their day to day dealings with the publishing world.

A good agent will read your manuscript with a critical eye, often suggesting minor alterations in your characters or storylines, before offering your manuscript for sale. Theirs is a valuable skill and their advice should not be disregarded. Together an author and agent can become a successful team, each providing a benefit for the other.

Once again, market research provides the key to tracking down an agent who might be prepared to consider representing your interests. *The Writers' & Artists' Yearbook* features a list of literary agents, including details of the type of material each one handles. Only approach agents who, to your certain knowledge, have other children's authors on their books. By so doing, you will not only increase your chances of acceptance but will also ensure that you are placing your trust in someone who is qualified to market your material within your chosen field.

Having selected a suitable agent, the next step is to persuade them to act for you. Your initial approach must be carefully designed to make a good first impression as it is on this, as much as the manuscript itself, that you will be judged. Agents work on a close personal level with their clients and if they foresee a potential clash of personalities or interests, this will colour their judgement as much as the quality of your manuscript.

They also look for earning potential in their clients, and only if they can see plenty of mileage in your work will they be prepared to consider taking you on board.

The negotiation and subsequent sale of your manuscript will undoubtedly involve the agent in a degree of expenditure. He must consider the costs involved in staffing his office, in postage, telephone costs, photocopying, stationery and of course, entertaining both clients and publishers. If these costs are to be offset against the income he will derive from the author, then that author must have a potential minimum earning power of between £15,000 and £20,000 p.a.

It is unlikely that this level of income will be achieved with the sale of a few short stories or even a number of regular commissions by a handful of children's publishers. Once the relationship between the agent and the author of children's books has been established, however, the agent may be prepared, if the author so wishes, to negotiate lesser works such as short stories and articles on his or her behalf. Initially, however, these items would not be of sufficient interest to encourage an agent to act for you.

APPROACHING AN AGENT

Many novice authors tremble at the thought of lifting the telephone and asking for an editor, publisher or agent by name, yet often, particularly in the case of initial contact with an agent, it is the best route to take. But do get your act together before you make that call. Agents are busy people and you will need to be able to outline your idea clearly and without unnecessarily long explanation. By establishing a personal contact in this way, should the agent show sufficient interest to ask that you send the manuscript without delay, then you can be sure that it will be read.

For an author who prefers to make the initial approach in writing, however, agent Caroline Sheldon offers the advice that your manuscript should be accompanied by a covering letter briefly outlining the content of your book and giving a short résumé of your writing experience to date. The letter should be informative but should cover no more than one, or at most two, A4 sheets of paper. The manuscript should, of course, be neatly presented in a card folder, as outlined in Chapter Eleven.

One of the things that agents have in common with publishers is that they also have a slush pile – a quantity of manuscripts waiting to be read. Under no circumstances be tempted to harass the agent into making a decision. It may take several weeks before you know whether or not he is prepared to act on your behalf.

A good agent will earn every penny of the ten percent he receives from your income. Sadly, not all agents fall into this category, as many a well known author has learned to their cost. Some, for example, will demand a reading fee before they are prepared to look at your manuscript. Once again, opinion is divided about this: if such a fee is payable, then it should be safe to assume that your manuscript will be given a thorough and detailed examination and that any written criticism will be comprehensive.

On the other hand, consideration should be given to the fact that your manuscript may be skimmed through and a criticism with little value offered to the writer. Should this be the case, then it must be acknowledged that this sort of service can be both costly and ineffective. The majority of good agents have no need to charge a fee for reading. While an agent is constantly searching for new talent to include in his list of clients, it may well be that the list is full when your manuscript arrives on his desk. He can, after all, only provide a truly excellent service for a specific number of clients. To increase that number would reduce the quality of the service.

So if your manuscript is returned, do not lose heart; try again with a different agent. Eventually, if your work is good enough, you will find someone who will share with you the conviction that your work is saleable.

SYNDICATION

Having said earlier that, if you established a good relationship with your agent he may be prepared to negotiate the sale of short stories and articles, it should be noted that there are agents who specialise in the syndication of these smaller items.

The function of a syndication agent is to sell the same item – comic strips, articles or short stories – to a number of different publications both at home and overseas. The advantage to the writer lies in the savings on postage, telephone and record keeping, plus the agency's knowledge of and contact with a wide range of receptive outlets.

The possible disadvantage, however, is that in some cases the percentage taken by the agent can be excessive. It is advisable to deal only with a reputable syndication agency, specialising in your field, and at the outset to establish the percentage they intend to deduct from any sales.

It is also worth remembering that once an agency has negotiated a contract with several publications requiring that you, the author, produce for example, a regular weekly column, then it is imperative that you are capable of delivering your copy with proper regularity throughout the duration of the contract.

RECORD KEEPING

Record keeping is something which should be done from the outset of your career as a writer, and initially it does not need to be complicated. A simple exercise book will suffice with each double page ruled into seven columns.

In column 1, each entry should be numbered for your reference. The second column should be headed 'Date' and will register the date upon which you despatch your manuscripts. The next column should be headed 'Title', beneath which should appear details of the relevant manuscript, its length and format – short story, article etc. The fourth column should specify the name and address of the publisher to whom the manuscript has been sent. Column 5 is reserved for the result of your submission, the date of its rejection or acceptance. Should the latter be the case, then column 6 should list the fee received and the seventh and last column should clearly specify the rights sold.

An ideal method of cross reference is that of the card index system. Each card should be headed with the title of the short story, article or book, followed by its approximate length. Listed below that should be the names and addresses of the publishing houses to which it has been submitted, accompanied by the relevant reference number in your book. Again, details of rejections or acceptances should be noted on the card and the whole system kept up to date on a weekly basis.

A system of this nature will enable you to trace the whereabouts of a manuscript easily and to keep month by month track of your income.

EXPENDITURE

The question of recording expenditure is a matter of commonsense. From the outset of your career as a writer, any expenses should be meticulously noted and receipts from any purchase connected with writing should be numbered and filed in date order.

Once again, a simple exercise book will suffice, ruled into columns in a similar manner, bearing such headings as 'Reference Number', 'Date' and 'Expenditure Details'. Expenditure details can include postage, telephone, travel, research, periodicals, stationery, subscriptions and any writing courses which contribute towards your professional skills.

Whilst your early income may be minimal, the keeping of these records is essential. Eventually, your income may run into larger annual amounts and the taxman will require well kept records.

Be sensible about the amounts you attempt to claim as expenditure. Expensive business lunches with editors, for example, would probably be disallowed, as would any similarly questionable claims. Under normal circumstances, the tax inspector will allow a proportion of the cost of running your home, that is to say, lighting, heating, telephone rental etc.

Whilst on the subject of dealing with tax inspectors, bear in mind that it would be foolish to think that you can omit from your records any incoming payment in the hope they might pass unnoticed. Remember that the bookkeeping of every publishing house is open to the scrutiny of the Tax Office and will certainly log their payment to you.

DO YOU NEED AN ACCOUNTANT?

The wise writer, having reached the stage of receiving a fairly regular income from their work, will seek the services of an accountant, preferably one who has experience in this particular professional area. You must become established, in the eyes of the tax authorities, as a self-employed writer and as your income grows, be sure to set aside, at your accountant's recommendation, a percentage of your income against the inevitable tax demand. From the outset, writing should be regarded as a business enterprise and income and expenditure should be managed accordingly.

A number of leaflets can be obtained from the Inland Revenue, giving you details of what is and what is not tax deductible. You should open a separate bank account for your earnings from writing and keep full records of all financial transactions with copies of correspondence and everything you have published.

The tax authorities are well aware that professional free-lance writers may also be in alternative full-time employment, but earnings on the basis of self-employment as a writer are taxed separately. For tax purposes, you will be assessed on your total annual income. Be aware that initially you may not be accepted by the tax authorities as a professional writer but once your book has been sold, royalties will be liable and you should be able to claim back expenses incurred in writing the book.

As soon as you begin to earn money from your writing on a regular basis the Department of Social Security should be notified as you may be required to pay National Insurance contributions. The Inland Revenue will give you details of your tax threshold (ie: the amount you are permitted to earn in a year before you are liable for tax) and if it is clear you are approaching this sum then you should think about consulting an accountant.

Perhaps the best way to go about this is by recommendation, particularly from a fellow writer, as your financial affairs will best be handled by someone conversant with the specific tax problems of royalty payments, advances and so on. A large one-off payment, for example, may be spread across several years for tax purposes, and professional advice becomes vital.

Do not, however, be afraid to shop around for reasonable rates. Large firms may be expensive and possibly lack that personal touch that the inexperienced writer finds so comforting when coping with financial matters. A small, one-man band, however, may offer more reasonable rates but lack the necessary expertise you require.

In some cases, if your initial earnings are relatively low, a sympathetic accountant may be prepared to look at your finances on a one-off basis, just to get you started. As your income will almost certainly fluctuate from one year to the next, once he has a rough idea of the amounts involved, he will tell you honestly whether it is worth your while employing his services or whether you can safely submit your own figures direct to the Inland Revenue.

As soon as you find yourself dealing with large sums which might require VAT registration, then professional advice is essential. VAT is payable on royalties and advances to authors, agents' fees, stationery and most capital equipment. As soon as you have reason to believe that your income will exceed the registration limits, which are increased roughly in line with inflation, then you must register for VAT. Your publisher would normally pay VAT on top of your regular advance or royalties and VAT is deductible from all your outgoings.

Income, for the majority of children's writers, is at best patchy and at worst, non-existent. Only a relatively small minority achieve financial security from their work but the income they do derive must be carefully managed if it is not to be lost in payments to the tax authorities. The rule, therefore, should be that when in doubt, consult an expert.

USEFUL ADDRESSES

The addresses of most children's publishers will be found in the *Writers' & Artists' Yearbook.*

The Penguin Group has in recent years acquired many well known children's publishing houses in addition to their own children's paperback imprint, Puffin Books. They are at 27 Wrights Lane, London W8 5TZ (Tel: 071-416 3000). Puffin Books publish mainly reprints, fiction, poetry, picture books and some non-fiction in their *Young Puffin Factbook* series. Other Puffin series include *Picture Puffins* for the pre and primary school markets, *Puffin Plus* for the young teens and *Young Puffins*, first readers for younger children.

The following publishing houses are subsidiaries of the Penguin Group: Blackie Children's Books; Fantail; Hamish Hamilton Children's Books; Viking Children's Books; Frederick Warne.

Another major group in the children's publishing world is Transworld Publishers Ltd, 61–63 Uxbridge Road, London W5 5SA (Tel: 081-579 2652). Transworld imprints include: Bantam; Corgi paperback fiction; Picture Corgi (picture books for pre and primary school children); Young Corgi (paperback first readers); Doubleday; Freeway; Yearling.

Other reputable publishing houses include:

A&C Black Publishers Ltd, 35 Bedford Row, London WC1R 4JH (Tel: 071-242 0946).

Hamlyn Children's Books, 38 Hans Crescent, London SW1X 0LZ (Tel: 071-581 9393).

HarperCollins Publishers, 77–85 Fulham Palace Road, Hammersmith, London W6 8JB (Tel: 081- 741 7070). Imprints include Dinosaur.

Hodder & Stoughton Ltd, 47 Bedford Square, London WC1B 3DP (Tel: 071-636 94851).

Longman Group Ltd, Longman House, Burnt Mill, Harlow, Essex CM20 2JE (Tel: 0279 426721).

Methuen Children's Books, 38 Hans Crescent, London SW1X 0LZ (Tel: 071-581 9393).

Pan Macmillan Children's Books Ltd, 18–21 Cavay Place, London SW10 9PG (Tel: 071-373 6070).

Random House UK Ltd, 20 Vauxhall Bridge Road, London SW1V 2SA (Tel: 071-973 9720).

Usborne Publishing, Usborne House, 83–85 Saffron Hill, London EC1N 8RT (Tel: 071-430 2800).

Many publishers now include a number of series books in their lists including the following:

A&C Black (Publishers) Ltd, 35 Bedford Row, London WC1R 4JH:

Jets (2,500 words for 6–8 year olds; black/white illus on every page).

Jumbo Jets (4,000–5,000 words for 7–9 year olds, black/white illus on every page).

Blackie Children's Books, 7 Leicester Place, London WC2H 7BP:

Blackie Bears (2,500 words for 5–7 year olds, black/white illus on every page).

Story Factory (6,000–8,000 words for 6–8 year olds, black/white illus).

Hamish Hamilton Children's Books, 27 Wrights Lane, London W8 5TZ:

Antelopes (7,500 words for 6–9 year olds, black/white illus).

Cartwheels (1,000 words for 4–8 year olds, full colour picture books).

Gazelles (2,500 words for 5–8 year olds, black/white illus).

Hodder & Stoughton, 47 Bedford Square, London WC1B 3DP:

Hedgehogs: (1,000 words for 4–7 year olds, full colour illus).

Pan Macmillan Children's Books, Cavage Place, London SW10 9PG:

Flippers (Two back-to-back 1,250 word stories for 6–9 year olds, black/white illus).

Viking Children's Books, 27 Wrights Lane, London W8 5TZ:

Kites (7,500–8,000 words for 7–9 year olds, black/white illus).

Read Alone (2,000–3,000 words for 6–8 year olds, black/white illus on every spread).

Series books for older readers:

In common with Puffin's Puffin Plus and Puffin Classics, several publishers offer series books directed specifically at the teenage market:

Transworld Publishers Ltd, 61–63 Uxbridge Road, London W5 5SA:
Bantam (Romantic fiction under a variety of series headings plus serious fiction for teenagers in the Young Adult list).
Pan Macmillan Children's Books:
Pan Horizons (Romantic fiction for teenagers).

Literary agents

Abacus Literary Agency, 298 Manchester Road, West Timperley, Altrincham, Cheshire WA14 5NB (Tel: 061-962 9749) Partners: Cliff South, Diane Parker. Early readers; children's adventure.
Curtis Brown, 162–168 Regent St, London W1R 5TB (Tel: 071-872 0331). Children's books and associated rights.
Juvenilia, Avington, Winchester, Hants SO21 1DB (Tel: 0962 78656) Proprietor: Mrs Rosemary Bromley. Full-length manuscripts for the children's market, fiction and non-fiction.
Caroline Sheldon Literary Agency, 71 Hillgate Place, London W8 7SS (Tel: 071-727 9102). Children's books.

Character merchandisers

Michael Woodward Creations, Parlington Hall, Parlington, Aberford, W Yorks LS25 3EG (Tel: 0532 813913) New concepts and characters needed.
Paul Lamond Games Ltd, Riverside House, 21–22 Colebrooke Row, Islington, London N1 8AP (Tel: 071-359 7271).

Children's literary awards

The Children's Book Award, given to authors of works of fiction published in the UK. Details: Jenny Blanch, 30 Senneleys Park Rd, Northfield, Birmingham B31 1AL.
Smarties Prize for books for children of primary school age. Prizes of £2,000 to each of three category winners plus £8,000 to overall winner. Details: The Book Trust, Book

House, 45 East Hill, London SW18 2QZ (Tel: 081-870 9055).

Whitbread Literary Award, five categories including Children's Novel. Writers must have lived in Great Britain and Ireland for three or more years. Submissions from publishers only.

Literary organisations

The Society of Authors has a subsidiary organisation for children's authors, the Children's Writers and Illustrators Group, 87 Drayton Gardens, London SW10 9SB (Tel: 071-373 6642).

The Association of Authors' Agents, 79 St Martins Lane, London WC2N 4AA (Tel: 071-836 4271) Secretary: Sara Fisher.

Children's Book Foundation, Book Trust, Book House, 45 East Hill, London SW18 2QZ (Tel: 081-870 9055).

The Writers' Guild of Great Britain, 430 Edgware Road, London W2 1EH (Tel: 071-723 8064-5-6).

Useful publications

The Writers' & Artists' Yearbook, A&C Black.

The Writers Handbook, Macmillan.

The World of Children's Books by Michelle Landsberg, Simon & Schuster.

Other books in *Writers News* series.

ACKNOWLEDGEMENTS

The author and publishers gratefully acknowledge the following for permission to reproduce copyright material in this book in the form of extracts taken from the following books and comics:

Forgive and Forget by David S. Williams, Pan Heartlines
Hot Dog and Other Poems by Kit Wright, Puffin Books
The Borrowers by Mary Norton, J.M. Dent & Sons Ltd
The Fib and Other Stories by George Layton, Collins
    Publishing Group
The Haunted Canal by Margaret Nash, Young Puffin
The Peppermint Pig by Nina Bawden, Victor Gollancz Ltd
Stig of the Dump by Clive King, Penguin Books Ltd
Twinkle Comic D.C. Thomson & Co Ltd
Mandy & Judy D.C. Thomson & Co Ltd

INDEX

Pratchett, Terry, 142, 146
Pre and Primary School
 Markets, 38
Pre natal contact, 23
Pre school comic, 38
Presentation, 90
Pretty Polly, 136
Prizes, obtaining, 166
Problems, 77, 82
Professional reading agency,
 88
Pseudonym, 92
Publishing contract, 99
Puffin, 40, 42, 133, 136,
 146, 148
Pullman, Philip, 148
Puns, 20, 54, 132

Racial prejudice, 20
Racism and Minority
 Groups, 147
Railway Children, 17
Rainbow, 104
Ransome, Arthur, 140
Raphael, Caroline, 160
Read alone books, 39
Realism, 32, 119, 142
Record Keeping, 94, 174
Recorded delivery, 94
Rejection, 96
Reviews, 165
Rhyme Stew, 134
Riding Hood, 67
Rights, 98
Romantic fiction, 32
Rosen, Michael, 132
Run Swift Run Free, 147
Run With The Wind,
 147

Sarcasm, 20
Satire, 132
School, 28
School stories, 28
Script layout, 108, 158
Self-employed writer, 176
Sendak, Maurice, 123
Serial, 113
Series books, 39
Sewell, Anna, 141
Sharratt, Nick, 132
Sheldon, Caroline, 172
Short story, 37
Shortlist, 43
Schuster, Joe, 120
Siegel, Jerry, 120
Simmons, Posy, 133
Six and upwards, 28
Slang, 54
Smith, W.H., 149
Snapshots, 103
Soap Star, 144
Social deprivation, 20
Social pressures, 85
Society of Authors, 99
Solution, 77, 87
Specialist ideas, 43
Sporting stories, 146
Stage, Writing for The,
 156
Stereotypes, 72
Stevenson, R.L., 141
Stig of the Dump, 14
Story book, 135
Storyline, 106
Study your reader, 25
Subsidiary rights, 98
Superman, 120
Sutcliff, Rosemary, 86

If you are serious about writing, join WRITERS NEWS. It is by far the best selling and largest magazine in the field, and has a hugely enthusiastic readership. The decision to join could be one of the best things you could do for yourself. Bring out your creativity and individuality... and of course supplement your income.

ALWAYS A FRIEND

Join WRITERS NEWS and you will never again be on your own. You will enjoy sharing the experiences of others and the comradeship of our own extensive competitions, answers to individual questions, correspondence columns and so on. Many readers tell us they drop everything else when the new issue drops through the letterbox and enjoy WRITERS NEWS as well as benefiting from its extensive coverage of the issues that affect writers.

WIDE COVERAGE

From the electric desk top to finance, and copyright to legal matters, we're there to help. Tax, royalty agreements, stylistic matters, research sources, finding an agent or publisher, self-publishing – we routinely bring you up to date in a very accessible manner. Richard Bell, our editor, likes to think that the magazine belongs to its readers and is influenced by what they want.

HELPLINE

And where we are not specific enough for your individual circumstances, we will advise you personally in our popular Helpline which has experts in all fields of writing and publication waiting to answer your questions. WRITERS NEWS belongs to its readers. Make it *your* source of help.

ALL KINDS OF WRITING

Short stories, novels, articles, non-fiction books, children's, poetry, religious writing, technical writing... every kind is covered by our formidable team of regular contributors (there is of course also scope to contribute the one-off article) with points of substance, style and marketing... just about everything you could expect and more.

MARKET NEWS

While writing just for personal enjoyment can be a great hobby, our primary purpose is to see you get published and our columns bulge with news of market opportunities – of all kinds; fiction and non-fiction, the broadcast as well as the written word. The service provided by a team of reporters is unique – both informing you of important events and trends *and* providing you with news of specific opportunities.

TWO MAGAZINES IN ONE

WRITERS NEWS, available only by postal subscription, comes with the up-to-date inside story each month. Five times a year it is joined by WRITING MAGAZINE (also available on the newsstands) to give you the most complete, in-depth coverage possible. Your subscription brings well over 700 fact and advice-packed pages... about five pence per page... and each one has the potential to open new horizons.

COMPETITIONS, COMPETITIONS

Many people join especially for our unique range of competitions, nearly all winners being published (and sometimes given a critique by famous writers). As a subscriber you enjoy free entry to at least one competition each month, while at least once a quarter there is a £1,000 top prize for a short story competition with a nominal entry fee... all exclusive to WRITERS NEWS. There is also an annual short story competition for the year's new subscribers also with a £1,000 top prize.

KEEPING IN TOUCH

To emphasise readers' involvement, we will of course also tell you of other people's competitions and about writing seminars, courses, special weekends and awards and allowances. A directory of local writers' circles and of professional organisations for writers are just two of the annual reference supplements included within WRITERS NEWS.

AND IT'S GREAT FUN!

Writing is a very human business and our letters page, columns, quizzes, news pages, even our 'Personals', are often as much fun as they are instructional. It is no wonder that so many say that WRITERS NEWS is their *favourite magazine*.

– Subscription form overleaf

Join the many thousands who write better and more profitably!

WRITERS NEWS SUBSCRIPTION FORM

(PHOTOCOPIES WILL BE ACCEPTED)

Name ....

Address ....

....

.... Postcode ....

Have you previously subscribed or applied to subscribe? Yes/No

PLEASE TICK AND COMPLETE A, B OR C BELOW

Those opting for A or B enjoy a discount of £5 off the annual subscription currently £39.90-£5 = £34.90 (Europe inc Eire £49.90-£5 = £44.90: rest of the world £54.90-£5 = £49.90). 1994 prices.

☐ A. DIRECT DEBIT

Payment instruction to bank/Building Society
Originators Identification No: 930895

1. To the Manager .... Ref No ....

.... Bank/Building Society

2. Account in the Name of ....

3. Account No. ☐☐☐☐☐☐☐☐   Sort code ☐☐–☐☐–☐☐

4. Instruction to Bank/Building Society
● I instruct you to pay Direct Debits from my account at the request of **WRITERS NEWS LTD.**
● The amounts are variable and may be debited on various dates. I understand that **WRITERS NEWS LTD** may change the amounts and dates only after giving me prior notice.
● I will inform you in writing if I wish to cancel this instruction.
● I understand that if any direct debit is paid which breaks the terms of this instruction, you will make a refund.

5. Signed .... Date ....

☐ B. CREDIT CARD (Visa or Access/Mastercard)

I authorise you to debit my credit card with the annual subscription on receipt and annually thereafter on the same date unless cancelled by me.

1. Please tick box   ☐ Visa   ☐ Access/Mastercard

2. Card Number ☐☐☐☐☐☐☐☐☐☐☐☐☐☐☐☐

3. Expiry Date ....

4. Signed .... Date ....

☐ C. CASH

1. I prefer to pay by Cheque/Postal Order and send £39.90 (Europe inc Eire £49.90: rest of the world £54.90). 1994 prices.
Cheques should be made payable in sterling to: WRITERS NEWS LTD

2. Signed .... Date ....

Return the completed form to:
WRITERS NEWS LTD, PO Box 4, Nairn IV12 4HU
(Phone 0667 454441 Fax 0667 454401)

WLV8

WRITERS BOOK SOCIETY

Increase your creativity and save a small fortune! Aiming to provide the very best in practical, reference and other books for writers from a wide variety of publishers, Writers Book Society is used by its members as their own bargain postal bookshop.

We are trying to bring you the best books in this rather specialised field, together with the convenience of shopping by mail-order. From the comfort of your own home you can peruse the available titles at your leisure – somewhat preferable to rooting around at the back of a bookshop for a title which will probably have to be specially ordered.

Writers Book Society sees the full, efficient and continued good service of its members as being integral to its success – and tries at all times to satisfy its customers. Any suggestions from members for titles which they feel appropriate for the club are most welcome.

For further details, please complete and return the coupon on page 192.

To Richard Bell, Principal,
Writers News Home Study Division,
PO Box 4, Nairn IV12 4HU

Please send me a prospectus

Name (BLOCK CAPITALS PLEASE) ....

Address ....

.... Postcode ....

☐ Please tick if you are a subscriber to Writers News   WLV8

£10 DISCOUNT FOR WRITERS NEWS SUBSCRIBERS

We are steadily adding to the advantages of subscribing to *Writers News*. One is that you save £10 on each of our home study courses. Save it until you come to pay for the course, having first requested the prospectus. Then you may treat this voucher as cash either against payment of the outright fee or the first instalment if you choose the instalment plan. Please sign.

I am a subscriber to Writers News and therefore claim the £10 reduction.

Signed ....

WLV8

To: Writers Book Society, PO Box 4, Nairn IV12 4HU

Please send me details of the latest introductory offer.

Name (BLOCK CAPITALS PLEASE) ....

Address ....

.... Postcode ....

☐ Please tick if you are a subscriber to Writers News   WLV8